Reading Strategy Lessons

for Science & Social Studies

15 Research-Based Strategy Lessons
That Help Students Read and Learn From Content-Area Texts

Laura Robb

■SCHOLASTIC

New York • Toronto • London • Auckland • Sydney
Mexico City • New Delhi • Hong Kong • Buenos Aires

Dedication

For my grandchildren, Lucas Benjamin and Helena Sylvie-Rose, with love

Acknowledgments

My sincere thanks to Dick Bell, history teacher at Powhatan School in Boyce, Virginia, and deeply respected colleague. I greatly appreciate your work on primary sources, as well as our many conversations about content learning and teaching and our shared teaching experiences.

A hearty thanks to all of the middle school students and science and social studies teachers at Powhatan School, at Shelburne Middle School in Staunton, Virginia, and at Johnson Williams Middle School in Berryville, Virginia. Your willingness to try these strategies and offer feedback provided me with material to revise and refine the lessons in the book and choose those that students believed were most helpful.

Special thanks to my editors, Virginia Dooley and Joanna Davis-Swing, who supported me through this project with astute suggestions and wise editing of the proposal; my deepest thanks for Joanna Davis-Swing for her thoughtful editing of the manuscript, for her patience, for her understanding of this topic and the purpose of the book, and for her positive editing style.

To all the history and science teachers I've worked with outside of Virginia, my thanks for permitting me to share your expertise, your ideas, and your classrooms.

To my husband, Lloyd, my thanks for your unflagging support and for your understanding of the time it takes to conceive of, write, and revise a book.

Credits: "Drip Dry" by Sean Price in *Science World*, April 18, 2005, Vol. 61, No. 13. Reprinted with permission. "Lewis and Clark: Journey Into the Unknown" by Matt Warshauer in *Junior Scholastic*, November 10, 2003, Vol. 106, No. 7. Reprinted with permission. *Interior Images:* faucet on p. 74: © Furnald/Gray/Jupiterimages; painting on p. 76: HULTONARCHIVE/GETTY IMAGES; portrait of William Clark on p. 76: © Bettmann/Corbis; map on p. 77: Jim McMahon/MAPMAN™; portrait of Meriwether Lewis on p. 77: © Bettmann/Corbis; painting on p. 78: © Hulton/Gettyimages; p. 93 (top): Library of Congress; p. 93 (bottom): University of North Carolina at Chapel Hill; p. 94: University of North Carolina at Chapel Hill; p. 95: Atlanta History Center

Cover design by Maria Lilja

Interior design by Sarah Morrow

Interior photographs by Bonnie Forstrum Jacobs

Copyright © 2009 by Laura Robb

All rights reserved. Published by Scholastic Inc.

Printed in the U.S.A.

ISBN-13: 978-0-439-92642-3

ISBN-10: 0-439-92642-4

2 3 4 5 6 7 8 9 10   40   15 14 13 12 11 10 09

Contents

Introduction

I wrote this book keeping in the forefront of my mind that science and social studies teachers want and need to teach content. Content and related vocabulary are what's required to think, speak, and write about a topic. In his keynote address at the 2006 Colorado Council International Reading Association (CCIRA) Conference in Denver, Colorado, researcher P. David Pearson said, "Subject matter is primary." Pearson called for the teaching of reading and writing skills and strategies to "buddy up" with subject content, making sure that the emphasis was on the information and thinking with the information rather than on the strategy or skill.

In this book, I've tried to achieve a balance for science and social studies teachers by providing short, focused, and easy-to-deliver lessons within the research-tested three-part learning model, which describes what happens before, during, and after reading. You'll find lessons that build students' prior knowledge and vocabulary and prepare them to read and learn. You'll explore strategies that enable students to self-monitor what they do and don't understand as they read, as well as several fix-up strategies that help students construct meaning when a passage confuses them. The after-reading activities invite students to discuss, think about, and analyze information, and encourage them to write to deepen their understanding. Remember, these lessons are short and focused because helping your students learn content is the primary focus of this book.

The last chapter discusses the use of primary sources and poetry in social studies and science. My hope is that on days when you're not introducing a strategy or having students practice it, you will find a few minutes to read a poem or share a letter written by a soldier or have students study and learn from photographs. Doing this can make a topic come alive for students and enables them to connect the information to their own lives and to global issues related to the topic.

The fifteen lessons in this book can improve students' reading of the content you teach. With deeper comprehension, students can enlarge their vocabulary, recall more details, and use the information to build new understandings.

Laura Robb

CHAPTER 1

Helping Students Read the Text

How These Quick Lessons Support Learning Content

"Make it quick and easy; I have content to teach" are words I hear again and again when I ask science and social studies teachers, "What kinds of strategies and tools should I include in a book to help content-area teachers teach reading?" Content teachers are right—for them subject matter is primary. Without information and subject-related vocabulary, students can't think about a topic such as life in Mesopotamia or plant and animal cells. What confronts content teachers daily are classes of students who read at different instructional levels, with many reading three or more years below the grade level of materials they use. Teaching short, focused reading strategy lessons can help students who read up to one year below grade level unpack meaning and learn content and vocabulary from challenging texts.

As a reading teacher, my goal is to partner with content teachers so that both of us can provide reading support for students. Actually, I want to make your teaching life easier. I want your students to become more independent learners through the strategy mini-lessons you present and student practice, freeing you from writing information-packed notes on the board for students to copy.

You can help students get the gist of information in a chapter by having them preview and discuss the nonfiction features in their textbooks and nonfiction trade books—features such as sidebars, diagrams, photographs and captions, and maps. Previewing these features can build sufficient background knowledge about a topic so that students can read to learn on their own. You can also build students' prior knowledge by preteaching key vocabulary words and concepts they'll encounter in a chapter. Frontloading students with information and vocabulary before they read supports those reading a few months below the level of the textbook, enabling them to comprehend the information.

In addition, I've included 15 quick and easy strategy lessons that work with social studies and science texts and materials. These lessons allow you to offer a tool kit of reading and vocabulary strategies that support students as they read to learn and think about your subject.

The Importance of Reading to Learn From Textbooks and Informational Texts

Whether you're teaching social studies or science, there are many ways for students to learn information: experiments and observations in science, interviewing and studying primary sources in social studies, and watching videos in both subjects. In the middle grades and in middle and high school, though, students' main resource is often the textbook. Therefore, it's beneficial for students to learn and practice how to read a textbook or informational book to activate and enlarge their knowledge about a subject. Teaching students to do so is simple and can be integrated into your daily instruction.

For example, in science, partners or small groups of students can collaborate on a motivating hands-on activity in which they distinguish, sort, and classify the different kinds of minerals in a tray of rocks and then justify their decisions with facts, simple tests, and observations. Students will need to know vocabulary related to rocks as well as the kinds of tests scientists conduct to identify minerals—information from their textbooks. With the support of strategy lessons on reading nonfiction text features, using self-monitoring strategies, and taking notes, students are prepared to tackle this task successfully. In addition, when you structure learning this way, students grasp the importance of using textbooks as a resource for exploring a new topic. In other words, the activity motivates students to read to learn vocabulary and understand concepts. Instead of using you as the only source of knowledge, students learn to use their reading expertise to gather information from their textbooks, trade books, and other nonfiction materials. I would also point out that knowledge gathered through motivation and need has a better chance of moving to students' long-term memory than facts and terms memorized for a test.

Find alternate texts for students who read two or more years below grade level.

In social studies, students can connect their reading and discussions to an issue, such as global warming, or an essential question, such as *Is war inevitable?* When you introduce such big ideas, you're asking students to use the information gained from texts, videos, interviews, and primary sources to deepen their insights into an issue that extends beyond a particular historical period. Learning to deepen understanding of a core issue or problem adds relevance and meaning to the facts, encouraging more-thoughtful reading and thinking.

In the appendix (page 74), I've included some issues and essential questions for science and social studies topics you can use to help students learn the content they need to pass mandated tests. But even more important, these issues and questions can show students that science and social studies are subjects relevant to their lives.

As You Read On . . .

In Chapters 2, 3, and 4, you'll revisit the research-tested, three-part learning model and explore the strategies, lessons, and lesson formats introduced in this chapter. The Textbook Treasure Hunt (pages 11–13) is a good starting point as it familiarizes students with the organization of their textbooks and the nonfiction features found in them. The activity prepares students for reading to learn and enables them to more easily navigate their text because they know the features it contains and what they can learn from each one. I've also included a list of nonfiction text features along with short explanations for you to share and review with students.

This chapter closes with a discussion of the kinds of learning activities that motivate adolescents. In addition to a list of six characteristics of these learners, I've included a chart that lists the kinds of learning experiences appropriate for the high energy levels and critical-thinking abilities of this age group. The short strategy lessons not only enable you to help your students read to learn, but also include collaboration between pairs and among small groups.

The Three-Part Learning Framework

I've organized the strategy lessons around the research-tested, three-part learning framework, in which students prepare to read, monitor their learning during reading, and use the information learned in discussions and/or writing after reading. The chart below contains the strategies you'll explore in each part of this framework (Dowhower, 1999; Pearson, 2001; Robb, 2003, 2006; Tierney & Readence, 2000; Vacca & Vacca, 2000).

You might have to present a brief strategy lesson several times, thinking aloud during each presentation to show students how the strategy works. You can use your textbook, a trade book students are reading, or a read-aloud text to model a strategy. Your demonstration is the key to students' absorbing a strategy because it can develop students' mental model or visual picture of the strategy, how it works, and how it can support their comprehension and recall of information (Duke & Pearson, 2002;

A List of Strategies in the
Three-Part Learning Framework

STRATEGY LESSONS THAT PREPARE STUDENTS FOR READING AND LEARNING	STRATEGY LESSONS THAT BUILD COMPREHENSION DURING READING	STRATEGY LESSONS THAT SUPPORT RECALL AND UNDERSTANDING AFTER READING AND LEARNING
These lessons activate prior knowledge and support learning, especially when the topic is new.	*These lessons help students understand information while reading, show them how to self-monitor to discover what they do and don't comprehend, and help them start building vocabulary knowledge.*	*These lessons help students build new understandings, foster connections to other texts and issues, determine important information, and deepen students' recall and knowledge of new material and vocabulary.*
• List/Group/Label • Rate Your Word Knowledge • Preview/Connect/Question • Preteach Vocabulary to Build Concepts • Word Analysis Map	• Sticky Note Strategy • Read/Pause/Retell/Evaluate • Reread or Close Read • Using Context Clues to Build Vocabulary and Strategies for Pronouncing Words	• Word Map • Think With Heading Notes • Question/Answer/Connect/React • The 5 W's: Taking Notes and Writing Summaries • Collaborative Review Sheet • Forming a Hypothesis and Supporting It

Harvey & Goudvis, 2000; Pearson, Roehler, Dole, & Duffy, 1992; Robb, 2003, 2006; Tierney & Readence, 2000). In other words, the strategy lessons you present will show students how to read informational text and provide them with tools for learning from science and social studies materials. Once students absorb a strategy, they will naturally choose it when they need support to comprehend different texts.

About the Short, Focused Strategy Lessons You'll Explore

The strategy lessons in Chapters 2, 3, and 4 work smoothly in a 40- to 45-minute class period, taking only five to ten minutes—even less once you've presented them several times—and leaving most of your period for students to read, research, take notes, discuss material, write up experiments, study primary sources, complete quizzes and tests, and conduct experiments. Remember, helping your students learn content is the primary goal of this book.

The Elements of Each Strategy Lesson

The structure of all strategy lessons should be consistent, so students know what to expect each time you introduce a new strategy. A consistent structure also provides an easy-to-manage framework you can use to develop lessons for strategies not covered in this book. Here's what each strategy lesson includes:

- The Strategy's Name
- Purpose
- Materials
- Time
- Guidelines for Presenting the Lesson
- After Reading and Discussing
- Following Up

How to Use This Book

I've limited the number of strategies to those most essential for students to learn content from their textbook and other materials. My suggestion is that you read through the strategies in each part of the before, during, and after learning/reading framework and choose one strategy from each part that you feel will be most helpful to your students. Next, work through a lesson by introducing a chapter or unit with the before-reading strategy you selected. As you work through the chapter, offer students a during-reading strategy that helps them self-monitor and fix up comprehension. When you wrap up the chapter, select an after-reading strategy lesson that encourages reflection. To assist you in deciding which strategies to use, I highlight how each strategy supports students' learning.

Start your strategy instruction with whole-class presentations. Repeat a strategy lesson, modeling for the entire class, until all or part of the class understands the strategy. Remember, most of these lessons take ten minutes or less of class time; modeling the strategies and having students practice can help them read independently.

Work on the same set of strategies for three to four weeks, allowing time for students to observe you model, absorb by practicing, and then develop the confidence to apply the strategy while reading on their own. You'll know whether students "get it" by the questions they raise, by their responses to your questions, and by observing them practice the strategy in class.

TEXTS TO USE
WITH EACH
STRATEGY LESSON

Each strategy lesson can work with textbooks, magazine articles, trade books, Internet content, poems, and primary sources. For the model think-alouds and examples in this book, I've used a social studies article from Junior Scholastic, "Lewis & Clark: Journey Into the Unknown," by Matt Warshauer (pages 76–78), and a science article from Science World, "Drip Dry: Is It Possible That America's Water Sources Could One Day Be Tapped Out?" by Sean Price (pages 74–75).

In the last chapter, I discuss primary sources from different historical periods in American history. You'll find examples of primary sources on pages 93–95.

When students can discuss how the strategy works and explain why it's helpful to their learning, it's time to introduce another strategy. For example, it's possible that students understand the before- and after-reading strategies well, but still need more practice with self-monitoring and fix-up strategies. That's okay. Introduce one or two new strategies and continue practicing the one that requires more time. Avoid staying on a strategy more than five to six weeks. After six weeks, it's time to move on.

If a small group still needs extra practice, you can work with them while the rest of the class reads or writes, or you can pair them with a student who understands how to apply the strategy. If you plan to move on, make sure you tell the group that you'll be reviewing this strategy in a few months and that they will have additional practice at that time. Time away from a strategy often allows students' brains to absorb and apply it, and most will absorb it after the second or third revisit.

Teach Students Nonfiction Text Features

Since each chapter in your subject textbook will repeat specific features such as sidebars, a glossary of terms, or a list of key vocabulary words, it's helpful for students to understand how these features can support their learning. Below is a list of nonfiction features typically found in textbooks and other nonfiction. Not all the features will be in your textbook, and you and students might discover some features not on the list. The point is to invite students to collaborate to explore how each feature can support their reading and learning.

The question you're probably asking yourself now is *How do I familiarize students with these textbook features in as short a time as possible?* One enjoyable and quick way to do this is to start the year with a Textbook Treasure Hunt. You'll find the lesson for completing a Textbook Treasure Hunt on page 11; the student reproducible is on page 13.

Nonfiction Features

BIBLIOGRAPHY—You'll find this at the end of a book. The list cites the books and magazines the author used to research information for her book.

BOLDFACE TYPE—This is the darker type used for titles, headings, and key vocabulary. This feature calls readers' attention to words and phrases that are important.

DIAGRAMS—These are labeled illustrations of a process such as the water cycle or a visual of how something works such as the electric motor.

GLOSSARY—This alphabetic list at the back of the book contains the definitions of important and unusual words found in the text. Some glossary entries also include guidelines for pronouncing the word.

INDEX—This alphabetic list of key words, topics, and names of people and places in the text comes at the end of the book. Next to each item is a page number or several page numbers that refer the reader to a place in the book where the topic or person is mentioned. The more page numbers an index entry has, the more details you'll find about that topic.

INTRODUCTION—This part of a text can explain how the author conceived of the idea and often recognizes others who helped the author gather information.

MAPS—These help you locate a place the author discusses. With maps you can also follow the path of an explorer, pilot, or rescue effort.

PHOTOGRAPHS AND CAPTIONS—Photographs provide an image of an object or person; they can also give you information about a topic that's not in the text. Captions are one or two sentences that explain the photograph.

QUOTES AND INTERVIEWS—You'll find these features in sidebars or on a section of the page outside of the main text. Quotes or interviews give the exact words of a person or expert.

SIDEBARS—These boxes contain information that didn't quite fit in the text but that the author wanted to include. Sidebars can contain related information, quotes, part of an interview, a diary entry, a letter, or a newspaper clipping.

TABLE OF CONTENTS—At the front of a book, the table of contents lists chapter titles and page numbers. It provides a quick overview of what you'll find in the text.

TIMELINES—This feature can include important dates in a person's life, and can also present key dates from a historical period such as the Middle Ages or a major war such as the Civil War. Timelines can have photographs, illustrations, and short write-ups under each date.

Textbook Treasure Hunt

PURPOSE

To familiarize students with textbook organization and nonfiction features.

MATERIALS

Your subject-area textbook; the student reproducible on page 13.

TIME

Set aside 10 minutes a day for three consecutive days for pairs to complete the hunt.

HOW IT HELPS

The treasure hunt familiarizes students with the features in their science or social studies textbook. Knowing the nonfiction features repeated in each chapter (such as graphs, diagrams, photographs and captions, and charts) can help students use them to build background knowledge before reading and to set purposes for reading and learning. Students will find that they can skim parts of a textbook to locate information that answers questions and to find, review, and study details for quizzes and tests. In addition, the treasure hunt is a top-notch way to introduce teamwork and collaborative learning—instructional approaches that adolescent learners enjoy and that build their motivation to learn (Guthrie, 2004; Guthrie & Wigfield, 2000; Van Hoose & Strahan, 1988).

PRESENTING THE LESSON

1. Divide the class into teams of four students.

2. Give each team a reproducible to complete. Students should write their answers on a separate paper.

3. Have teams elect a scribe, the person who will record the answers, or choose a scribe yourself.

4. Have teams share with the class one or two items they've explored.

Enlist the Support of the English Teacher

If you're part of a grade-level team, you might want to ask the English teachers to help students recognize and understand how nonfiction features build background knowledge and prepare students to learn. When students read informational picture and chapter books in English class, their teacher will help them navigate these books by introducing the text features they'll meet. Students will quickly observe that the features they study in English are the same as those in their content textbooks.

This type of collaboration is beneficial to you and your students, especially if you plan to offer trade books to students at their independent-reading levels. Collaborating with the English teacher enables both of you to efficiently use class periods to teach nonfiction and at the same time provide students with information they need to be successful at reading and learning new content information.

Nonfiction Literature Matters

When students read texts that relate to a topic they're studying—on the Internet or in a book, newspaper, magazine article, or primary source—they can see information from multiple points of view, learn from materials they can read, and connect emotionally and intellectually to an event and topic. Using multiple sources (see also Chapter 5) can deepen and enlarge students' understanding of

Textbook Treasure Hunt

Directions: *Use your textbook to answer the questions below. Write your answers on a separate sheet of paper.*

1. Find and check out the index. Where is it? How many pages is it? Locate and jot down a topic that has several consecutive pages listed after it (there is information about that topic on each of the pages). Find and jot down a topic that has only a single page listed. What conclusions about the information on a topic can you draw from the number of pages that address it?

2. Look through the table of contents. Where is it located? How many chapters or units of study does it include? List three topics you would like to study. List five additional topics covered in this textbook.

3. Glance through the glossary. Where is it located? What information does a glossary contain? Select and jot down two words from the glossary that you know something about and two that are unfamiliar. How can the glossary help you understand the meanings of unfamiliar words?

4. Check out the first page of a chapter. List all the nonfiction features and information on that page.

5. List three boldface words in a chapter. Find out what each one means by reading around the word. Write the definition in your own words. What else can you use in the textbook to explore the meanings of words?

6. Skim the textbook and find a photograph. Note the page number. Study the photo and read the caption. Write, in your own words, what you learned. How can photos and captions help you understand new topics?

7. Find a graph, diagram, chart, and/or map. Note the page each feature is on. Now, study each one and read the print. In your own words, write what each feature can teach you.

8. Flip through two chapters. What other features do you find? How do these features help you learn new information?

9. Take a look at the last page or two of a chapter. What do you find there? How can these features help you learn information?

10. Skim through a chapter. Is there anything that confuses you? Note the page number and ask your group members to help you. If they can't help, then ask your teacher.

content area topics and vividly portray historical periods or scientific issues, engaging adolescent students and motivating them to learn. Before you plunge into the strategy lessons, take the time to read the next section and reflect on the nature and needs of the adolescents you teach.

Learning Activities for Young Adolescents That Match Their Developing Personalities

As you plan reading strategy instruction, consider the kinds of learning situations that motivate young adolescents to read, learn, observe, research, and study. To help you link the unique characteristics and needs of these students to the kinds of instructional situations you organize, it's helpful to first review six characteristics of this age group.

1. Students of this age have high energy levels and find it tough to sit still for long periods of time. They have varying attention spans, usually lasting no longer than 20 minutes.

2. *Who am I?* is a question students continually wrestle with as they struggle to carve out an identity and discover what they believe and value.

3. For students who experience success in school, positive self-concept and self-confidence levels can rise during these years. However, for those students who struggle to learn and read every day, self-confidence and self-esteem can reach all-time lows. Teachers see evidence of this diminishing self-confidence in poor behavior and negative attitudes toward learning and school.

4. For adolescents, peer opinions become more important than parental and adult opinions. Students' desire for peer approval is high, and standing apart and being different from the majority is often tough and unacceptable.

5. Students are developing the ability to think abstractly in all subjects.

6. Talk is what all of these students excel at. Being social, having friends, and being part of the "in" crowd is the goal of most.

Instructional Approaches That Engage Young Adolescents

When planning instruction in your science or social studies class, it's beneficial to consider the six characteristics of young adolescents listed above. Why? When you meet their learning needs as well as create instructional experiences that build on their strengths, you can motivate students to want to learn and to work hard to explore a topic or solve a problem.

The chart that follows offers you instructional approaches that build on the kinds of learning experiences that benefit adolescents (Beck & McKeown, 2006; Duke &

Organizing Teaching and Learning Experiences

DESIGN LESSONS THAT INCLUDE:	STUDENT EXPERIENCES THAT MATCH LESSON
ACTIVE LEARNING Hands-on tasks that ask students to do and build their own understandings; teachers convey that they value students' ideas, contributions, and thinking.	• problem solving • addressing issues • presenting dramas and simulations • presenting projects and book talks • thinking, inferring, and connecting concepts and facts • completing experiments
RELEVANT LEARNING Active learning through paired and small-group discussions and presentations leads students to link information to other texts and to community and world issues.	• discussing issues that link the past with the present • discussing to understand how this information applies to their lives, community, and world issues. • participating in think-pair-share and small-group discussions around issues, themes, problems, and finding relevance • fleshing out different points of view on topics and linking these to students' perspectives
COLLABORATIVE LEARNING Students interact with a partner or small group to construct meaning and new understandings and to problem-solve.	• participate in partner and group discussions • prepare group presentations of simulations and results of experiments • negotiating behavior guidelines with groups • collecting multiple perspectives and diverse ideas through collaborative problem solving and by reading multiple texts.

Pearson, 2002; Guthrie, 2004; Van Hoose & Strahan, 1988; Wilhelm, 2002; Zarnowski, 2006). Notice how experiences such as discussions, problem solving, exploring issues, dramas, simulations, and exploring multiple perspectives all tap into one or more of the six characteristics that adolescent learners exhibit.

These learning and instructional approaches place the responsibility for understanding content on the student. What I'm inviting you to do is shift from feeling that you must pass information on to students and, instead, ask them to be actively involved in their learning before, during, and after they read and study any topic.

Continue to Think About . . .

Before you move on to preparing your students to read, reflect on the questions that follow and think about your teaching style and how it meshes with the learning needs of adolescents.

- Do you frequently invite students to collaborate to solve problems, learn new vocabulary, help one another understand challenging texts, and study? Why is this beneficial?

- How do you make your content information relevant to students' lives?

- What strategies do you offer students to help them read to learn?

- What are examples of active and collaborative learning in your classroom?

- How do you know that students understand the nonfiction features they'll encounter in textbooks and nonfiction trade books?

16

CHAPTER 2

Before Students Read

Five Lessons That Build Background Knowledge and Vocabulary

The five strategy lessons in this chapter prepare students to read a text to learn about a topic. Researchers agree that the more prior knowledge students have about the topic and related vocabulary, the better their comprehension and recall will be (Alvermann & Phelps, 1998; Gillet & Temple, 2000; Harvey & Goudvis, 2000; Marzano, 2004; Readence, Moore, & Rickleman, 2000; Robb, 2003; Vacca & Vacca, 2000). I encourage you to quickly assess whether your students have adequate background knowledge to begin reading about a new topic. You can do this by asking them to brainstorm a list of what they know or by asking them to pair-share about a topic and discuss what they know. If students show that they have enough background knowledge and vocabulary to comprehend the reading material, then start your unit.

However, if students have little or no background knowledge and vocabulary, I urge you to invest time building their knowledge. Take five to ten minutes from a few class periods to enlarge their prior knowledge by showing video clips, looking at photographs, and reading short sections of texts. I always encourage teachers to find out what students know about a new topic approximately three days prior to the start of a unit of study.

This allows time for expanding students' background knowledge and vocabulary if necessary.

As You Read On . . .

In this chapter you'll explore five strategies that will prepare your students to read, comprehend, and recall what they've read: List/Group/Label, Rate How Much You Know About Words, Preview/Connect/Question, Preteach Vocabulary to Build Concepts, and Word Analysis Map. I've divided the chapter into two parts. The first part introduces each strategy and explains how it works as well as how the strategy helps students learn content. The second part contains brief lessons for each strategy with a think-aloud that introduces the strategy. Adapt these to the needs of your students. The chapter closes with questions that invite you to reflect on the importance of preparing your students to read and learn new vocabulary.

Five Before-Learning Strategies

In each lesson, I'll show you how the strategy works using the science text on pages 74–75 and the social studies text on appendix pages 76–78. An important step of each strategy lesson is to take a few minutes to make sure your students have specific purposes for reading and learning. Setting purposes helps students figure out which details are important to remember (Dowhower, 1999; Harvey, 1998; Keene & Zimmermann, 1997; Marzano, 2004; Readence, Moore, & Rickleman, 2000).

You'll want to integrate think-alouds into each strategy lesson you present to show students what's going through your mind as you read. As you think aloud and share how

Show Students How to Set Purposes on Their Own

Teachers are often the ones who set purposes for reading assignments. However, it's important for students to understand that having a purpose for reading helps them determine important details and understand the text better. Make this point explicitly to students and model how it works. Once students understand the benefits of setting purposes for reading and learning, show them how to do it on their own. Have students work with a partner so they can think it through collaboratively, and eventually they will have the self-confidence to set purposes independently. Pair students who can help one another; for those who read far below grade level, support them as a small group while others work together.

Students benefit from being able to set purposes on their own as they read texts independently for research, to solve a problem, or to learn more about a topic. Here are four suggestions for helping students set purposes—suggestions that move beyond the five strategies in this chapter.

Four Ways to Set a Purpose

1. **FIGURE OUT YOUR REASONS FOR OBSERVING AND MAKE THESE YOUR PURPOSES.**

   Science Example: To observe the effects of lack of sunlight on green plants.

2. **FORM A HYPOTHESIS, THEN SET UP AN EXPERIMENT IN SCIENCE OR DO RESEARCH IN SOCIAL STUDIES.**

   Science Example: Lowering gas emissions can slow down global warming.

   Social Studies Example: Misunderstandings and lack of communication lead to heightened tensions between nations.

3. **TURN THE CHAPTER TITLE AND HEADINGS INTO PURPOSES FOR READING.**

   Science Example: To learn how single-celled animals move, eat, and reproduce.

   Social Studies Example: To understand the influence of the Medicis on art and politics.

4. **THINK ABOUT THE TOPIC YOU'RE STUDYING.**

   Science Example: The topic is tracking tornadoes and hurricanes. The purpose can then be to discover how scientists track these storms and why tracking is important.

   Social Studies Example: The topic is the Boston Tea Party. The purpose for reading could be to discover what caused this event and how it affected the colonists and the British.

you complete and apply a strategy, you offer students the mental model they require to move to independence with a strategy. Woven into each strategy lesson, you'll find sample think-alouds for you to follow or adapt to your students' needs.

In the next section you'll find a brief introduction that explains each of the five strategies, followed by a description of how the strategy supports students' learning of your content.

1. List/Group/Label: Introduction

List/Group/Label activates the prior knowledge and vocabulary that students have about a topic by asking them to brainstorm anything they know. The strategy also asks them to group their ideas and then categorize the group with a label or heading, which helps them to analyze details. The strategy works best when students have some prior knowledge of a topic.

You can familiarize your students with nonfiction features by using the Textbook Treasure Hunt on page 13.

List/Group/Label: *How It Helps Students Learn Content*

This strategy supports and improves students' learning of information by:

■ enlarging students' background knowledge and vocabulary

- initiating analytical, high-level thinking by asking students to group and label items from their lists

- encouraging discussions between pairs that enlarge prior knowledge

- having students return to their original lists after reading, to review and to add new categories with related details

2. Rate Your Word Knowledge: Introduction

This strategy has students rate how much they know about a set of words before they read a text. Students rate four to eight words that you select from a text—words that are key to understanding and thinking about the topic. For each word, students independently decide whether they know a synonym for it or some characteristics of it, or whether the word is totally unfamiliar. Having this list enables students to set a purpose for reading, such as to learn more about these words and how they connect to the information in the text.

It's best not to grade this activity so that students will feel comfortable about figuring out their own level of knowledge. After reading and discussing the material, students can return to their knowledge rating charts and add what they've learned. Partners can work together and support one another, making the learning social and interactive.

Rate Your Word Knowledge: *How It Helps Students Learn Content*

This strategy supports and improves students' learning of vocabulary by:

- developing students' responsibility for learning new vocabulary

- enlarging their knowledge of new words and words they already know something about

- creating student investment in learning—they decide which words they need to learn more about

- focusing students on key words they'll encounter while reading

- asking students to return to their chart after reading and discussing the text and update it to reflect what they've learned about each word

- teaching students to be thoughtful about words and to recognize that understanding words affects comprehension and recall

3. Preview/Connect/Question: Introduction

This strategy builds students' background knowledge about a topic by asking them to analyze information highlighted in nonfiction text features such as headings, photographs and captions, diagrams, sidebars, and so on.

It's beneficial to move students beyond simply previewing the features to making two kinds of connections using the features. The first is to help students connect the information in the preview to what they already know. The second kind asks students to make connections among the features they're previewing. The process invites students to bring their personal experiences to the preview, including movies and TV programs they've watched; books, blogs, and Web sites they've read; and discussions they've participated in. As students make connections, they can use them along with details in the nonfiction features to wonder about the topic and raise questions, recording their questions on a journal page. These questions become students' purposes for reading the material. After reading, students can use their questions to discuss the text and take notes that respond to each query.

Preview/Connect/Question: *How It Helps Students Learn Content*

This strategy supports and improves students' learning of information by:

- having students engage with a text before they read in order to use and enlarge their background knowledge by making connections with nonfiction features

- helping students understand that nonfiction text features can support their comprehension and recall because these features outline key ideas and use new vocabulary

- asking students to raise questions that become their purposes for reading

- using their questions as a springboard for discussions and as a framework for taking notes

4. Preteach Vocabulary to Build Concepts: Introduction

Learning new information usually involves being exposed to new vocabulary and ideas. Therefore, it's important for students to have some background knowledge about words and concepts they'll need so they can understand new information. Pinpointing a concept and preteaching it along with key related words can help your students enlarge their vocabulary and understanding of the concept before reading.

First, choose the concept and three to six related words that you believe are essential for understanding the text. Introduce the concept and related words by writing them on chart paper, and pronouncing them if necessary. Next, have pairs preview the text and share what they know and have learned about the concept from nonfiction features such as photographs and captions, diagrams, maps, sidebars, or charts. Partners or groups record what they know on a Concept Map, grouping the words and related details that connect to the main word. Students share their maps so everyone receives the benefit of the knowledge classmates have.

At this point in the lesson, students will have heard and gathered information about several words they'll meet in the text. Now students are ready to read.

After reading and discussing the text, I recommend that you have pairs or small groups return to their Concept Maps, discuss the text and words, then add details to listed words as well as other words and details.

Preteach Vocabulary to Build Concepts: *How It Helps Students Learn Content*

This strategy supports and improves students' learning of vocabulary and concepts by:

- giving them some knowledge of words and concepts that can improve their reading comprehension and recall

- having them preview a text to enlarge their knowledge of a concept and related words

- incorporating paired discussions and whole-class sharing that broadens every student's knowledge of new words and concepts

- having students create a concept map that contains details and helps them organize their thinking about an idea and related words, which can give students a purpose for reading

5. Word Analysis Map: Introduction

This strategy invites students to work in pairs or groups, dip into their text, and read the sentence that contains the tough word. Pairs or groups collaborate to analyze the word from diverse perspectives such as noting its part(s) of speech, creating a context definition, noting its features, giving examples, and so on. You can preteach four to six words using the Word Analysis Map by organizing students into groups and giving each group a word; groups teach one another. You can also have each group complete a separate map for three to four words.

First, students write their word in the box at the top of the map. Next, each student reads the sentence that contains their word in the text being studied, then writes a definition based on context clues. Students might also have to read the sentences that come before and after the sentence with the tough word in it. In addition to giving examples, students also list situations in which they could use the word with writing or speaking, name the part(s) of speech, look up and discuss the dictionary definition of the word, and use the word in a sentence. Students use these words as purposes for reading—to find out more about each word's meaning and its relationship to the topic being studied. After reading and discussing, groups return to their maps and collaborate to refine their definitions, add situations and examples, and adjust their sentence, if necessary.

Word Analysis Map: How It Helps Students Learn Content

This strategy supports and improves students' learning of vocabulary by:

- asking them to read around a word and form a definition based on context clues and nonfiction features, which gets them into the text before reading and builds background knowledge of vocabulary

- having them find situations to use the word in and challenge them to craft original sentences

- broadening and deepening students' knowledge of the word prior to reading by listing other examples of the word or concept

- providing practice with looking up words in the dictionary

22

Five Lessons That Build Background and Vocabulary Knowledge

Work on one of these lessons for several weeks until students can complete the strategy with a partner, a small group, or independently. Then, introduce another strategy and practice it before moving on to yet another one. Choose the strategies you believe address the learning needs of the students you teach.

LESSON 1

List/Group/Label

PURPOSE

To build students' background knowledge and vocabulary; to show students how to group similar items, then categorize or label them

MATERIALS

"Drip Dry: Is It Possible That America's Water Sources Could One Day Be Tapped Out?" (pages 74–75); "Lewis & Clark: Journey Into the Unknown" (pages 76–78); or any topic to be studied in science or social studies; a class set of the List/Group/Label reproducible (page 80)

TIME

10 minutes on each of two consecutive days prior to or at the beginning of the unit; 10 minutes at the end of the unit

PRESENTING THE LESSON

1. Organize students into pairs.
2. Name the strategy and explain how it helps students learn information and why it's important for them to practice the strategy. Here's what I say:

   List/Group/Label invites you to talk to a partner to discover what you know about a topic. To gather more information about that topic and related vocabulary, you can preview your textbook or a magazine article by looking at the title, boldface headings, and photos or illustrations. It's also helpful to read captions and sidebars, and to study graphs, diagrams, and timelines. Write down a list of key words and phrases, important details, or interesting facts that you glean from the text during the preview. Then organize your list into groups of related ideas and give each group a label or heading.

This process helps you analyze and think with the information. These labeled groups become your purposes for reading and learning more about the topic; you read to find out more about the categories and confirm what you've written. Having prior knowledge and setting purposes for reading helps you pinpoint key details while reading and can improve your comprehension and recall of details. Returning to your original labeled groups at the end of the study enables you to adjust and add details; you can also create new groups of related information with headings and use these to review and study for tests and quizzes or to complete written work.

3. Introduce your topic by writing it on the board or by asking a question. For the science article, I write "America's Water Supplies" on the board. For the social studies article, I pose the question "What do you know about the journey of Lewis and Clark?" and write it on the board.

4. Next, invite students to preview their text by looking at the illustrations and reading the headings, sidebars, and captions, and by studying timelines, graphs, and diagrams.

5. Ask pairs to discuss their topic for two to four minutes and to think of words and phrases associated with it.

6. Have students write all the words, phrases, and ideas they can recall from their preview and discussion about the topic in their journals.

7. Invite students to share items from their lists, and record these on chart paper. Ask students to add to their lists words from the chart that are not in their journals.

    Here's the list of words and phrases that seventh graders generated for "America's Water Supplies":

drought makes worse	*scarce*
change saltwater to freshwater	*prevent pollution*
reverse greenhouse effect	*find ways to decrease wasting water*
prevent oil spills	*people use less water*
organic not chemical farming	*better appliances—use less water*

    Here's the list of words and phrases for "What Do You Know About the Journey of Lewis and Clark?" that fifth graders generated:

land of rivers	*Shoshone Indians*
Sacagawea, a guide	*exploration*
keelboat	*pirogues*
unknown territory	*an expedition*
made maps (cartography)	*food scarce*
safe food from land	*strenuous journey*
crossed more than half the U.S.	*needed guide to help*
Charbonneau, a guide	*kept diaries*

THE NEXT DAY

1. Model how you group a set of words under one heading or label; my think-alouds follow.

    THINK-ALOUD: "America's Water Supplies"
    I see some items that relate to prevention; I'll organize those into a group. (I write these on chart paper or the board.)

    *   *prevent pollution*
    *   *prevent oil spills*
    *   *people use less water*
    *   *better appliances—use less water*

    Let me reread these to think of a label or heading. (Reread.) *I think "Prevention Can Increase Water Supply" explains what these items are about, so that's what I'll write for my heading. I could also have just used "Prevention."*

    THINK-ALOUD: "What Do You Know About the Journey of Lewis and Clark?"
    I see items that have to do with this journey the explorers took; I'll write these on our chart. (Write items on chart.)

    *   *exploration*
    *   *unknown territory*
    *   *an expedition*
    *   *strenuous journey*
    *   *crossed more than half the U.S.*

    Let me reread the list. (Reread.) *Okay, I have two ideas for a label: "Exploring Unknown Lands" and "Expedition Into New Territory."*

2. Give partners a copy of the reproducible for List/Group/Label (page 80).

3. Ask pairs to organize the words and phrases from their lists on a separate sheet of paper. Then have pairs create a common heading for each group of details. Point out that some ideas might be under more than one heading. This is fine, as long as students can defend their choices.

4. Have pairs share a group and its label and explain the reasoning behind their choices.

SET A PURPOSE FOR READING—Read to discover more information about the groups and labels on your list. As you read, think of new groups and labels.

AFTER READING AND DISCUSSING

*   Have students add words and ideas to existing groups.
*   Invite pairs to create new groups based on their learning and label them.

FOLLOWING UP

- Model the strategy many times for students.

- Have partners practice this strategy before they read a new section of text. After three to four weeks, partners or individuals should be able to apply the strategy independently.

- Support students who still need your guidance and gradually move them to independence.

LESSON 2

Rate Your Word Knowledge

PURPOSE

To enlarge background knowledge and vocabulary; to develop students' responsibility for learning new vocabulary

MATERIALS

"Drip Dry: Is It Possible That America's Water Sources Could One Day Be Tapped Out?" (pages 74–75); "Lewis & Clark: Journey Into the Unknown" (pages 76–78); or any topic to be studied in science or social studies; list of selected words on a Rate Your Word Knowledge Chart (see page 80) or on chart paper; a class set of the Rate Your Word Knowledge Chart reproducible (page 80)

TIME

10 minutes before reading; 10 minutes after reading

PRESENTING THE LESSON

1. Name the strategy and explain how it can help students. Here's what I say:

   This strategy places you in charge of your learning because you decide which words you need to learn more about before you read assigned pages in a text. First, you'll rate what you do and do not know about each word on the chart I give you; you'll use these ratings to set purposes for reading. As you meet each word in the text, you'll learn more about its meaning and how it relates to the topic you're studying. After reading, you can work with a partner to discuss the words and add details under each heading on the chart. The more words you learn that relate to a topic, the better your recall of details and your ability to use information to draw conclusions and make connections.

2. Distribute the Rate Your Word Knowledge Chart to students. Write on chart paper the list of preselected words and have students write these words on the reproducible.

3. Ask students to rate their knowledge of each word.

4. Explain that this activity will not be graded; encourage students to be honest about their knowledge.

> SET A PURPOSE FOR READING—Read to discover more about words that are unfamiliar and words you know little about; as you read, try to discover the connections between these words and the topic you're studying.

AFTER READING AND DISCUSSING

- Have pairs or small groups discuss the words on their chart, using what they've learned from their reading.

- Ask individuals to add to their Rate Your Word Knowledge Charts details, based on their discussion and reading, that show what they've learned.

- Discuss the connections students made between the words and the topic they're studying.

FOLLOWING UP

- Ask pairs who need more support to help one another make corrections and add details to their charts after reading.

- Continue providing practice for the strategy and suggest to students that they can rate their knowledge about words that confuse them as they read on their own.

LESSON 3
Preview/Connect/Question

PURPOSE

To build background knowledge; to set purposes for reading by using the questions raised based on Preview/Connect/Question

MATERIALS

"Drip Dry: Is It Possible That America's Water Sources Could One Day Be Tapped Out?" (pages 74–75); "Lewis & Clark: Journey Into the Unknown" (pages 76–78); or any topic to be studied in science or social studies; a class set of the Journal Page reproducible (page 81)

TIME

10 to 15 minutes

PRESENTING THE LESSON

1. Introduce the strategy and explain how it helps students. Here's what I say:

   The strategy Preview/Connect/Question can build your knowledge of a topic before you read, which improves your understanding and recall of information. The strategy asks you to think about what you already know and connect it to photographs and captions, sidebars, headings, graphs, and any other nonfiction features you preview. You also make connections by linking information between and among features. Then you use your connections and details in the nonfiction features to pose questions. You'll use the questions you raise as purposes for reading, for discussions with classmates, and as a framework for taking notes that you can use to study for quizzes and tests.

2. Model how you use nonfiction features to preview the text and make connections to the topic. Note how I make clear when I'm connecting and when I'm asking questions. Two think-alouds follow: one using "Drip Dry" and the other "Lewis & Clark."

THINK-ALOUD: "Drip Dry"

The photo of dry, cracked land and the question at the top of the page—"Is it possible that America's water sources could one day be tapped out?"—remind me of the way our vegetable garden looked after six weeks of no rain along with restrictions on watering. On the third page of the article, I connect to the illustrations and headings because they make news headlines almost every day: water pollution and a decreasing water supply that can't support our growing population. I can connect the headings "Water World" and "Sustaining Supplies" to the fact that our world has more water than land, but sustaining drinkable water can be a problem. Here are questions I raise based on my preview and the nonfiction features: How can we sustain water supplies? How can people stop using so much water? How can fossil fuels affect water? What measures can be taken to prevent water pollution? Why does global warming affect water pollution?

THINK-ALOUD: "Lewis & Clark"

The illustration and caption, along with the subtitle "Journey Into the Unknown," make me think that Lewis and Clark are exploring territory that no white man has visited. I connect pirogues and keelboat to the heading "Starting Out" because both are boats the explorers used for the water part of the journey. I wonder what the author means in the second subhead—"Their journey would change the U.S. forever." That will be a question. When I skim the timeline I see that the journey took more than two years and is called "Voyage of Discovery." I can connect this to the map on the next page, which shows that the expedition covered more than half of the U. S. and "discovery" makes me wonder, What exactly did they discover? The heading "Chronicling the West" connects me to the word "cartographer," which lets me know that Clark made maps of all he saw. "America's Future" connects me to the fact that this journey changed our country forever. Here are the questions that the nonfiction features and my Preview/Connect raised: How did the journey of Lewis and Clark change the U.S. forever? What did they discover on this voyage and journey? Why did Lewis and Clark need the help of Native Americans? How did the Native Americans help them? What made the expedition grueling and treacherous? Why did the journey take so long?

---

3. Explain that there could be other questions and that that's fine as long as the questions come from information in the Preview.

4. Make sure students understand that they use the nonfiction features to raise questions along with their Preview/Connect. This will keep questions and information in the nonfiction features connected.

5. Show students how to set up a double-entry journal with their name, date, title, and pages (see page 81 for reproducible). Place questions on the left-hand side, skipping five to six lines between questions. Students will use the right-hand side for taking notes (see suggestions under the section "After reading and discussing").

Double-entry journal page

SET A PURPOSE FOR READING—Read to discover answers to the questions you've raised.

AFTER READING AND DISCUSSING

• Ask students to return to the questions they've written on the left-hand side of a journal page. Have students jot down notes, based on what they recall, next to each question.

• Tell students to skim the text for questions they feel need additional details to be answered fully. Have them add these notes in their own words.

FOLLOWING UP

• Have partners practice the strategy several times.

• Select students who can work with a partner independently on Preview/Connect/Question.

• Work with those students who would benefit from extra modeling and practice.

LESSON 4
Preteach Vocabulary to Build Concepts

PURPOSE
To enlarge knowledge of a concept and related vocabulary; to introduce a Concept Map

MATERIALS
"Drip Dry: Is It Possible That America's Water Sources Could One Day Be Tapped

Out?" (pages 74–75); "Lewis & Clark: Journey Into the Unknown" (pages 76–78); or any topic to be studied in science or social studies; preselected concepts and four to six related vocabulary words; a class set of the Concept Map reproducible (page 81)

TIME

10 minutes for partners or groups

PRESENTING THE LESSON

1. Introduce the strategy and explain how it enlarges vocabulary and supports reading comprehension. Here's what I say:

   The new topics you are learning about this year introduce unfamiliar words, and these words are important for developing an understanding of the topic and related concepts. To help you, I'm going to have partners (or small groups) complete a Concept Map for words you'll need to understand for an important concept that we're going to study. You'll work with a partner (or in a group) and preview the nonfiction features in the material you'll be reading—features such as illustrations and captions, sidebars, diagrams, and maps that can help you discover details about each related word. With your partner (or group), you'll add as many details as you can about each word based on what you already know and what you learned from the preview.

   After reading and discussing the text, you will adjust and add details to your map and share with classmates what you've learned. Your presentations will connect the concept and related words to the topic. The whole process will strengthen your understanding.

2. Organize students into pairs or small groups.

3. Give each pair or group a Concept Map to complete. Introduce the concept and the four to six related words you've selected, writing them on chart paper or the board. For "Drip Dry," I introduce the concept of water scarcity and these related terms: *air pollution, global warming, irrigation, fossil fuels, drought.*

   For "Lewis & Clark," I introduce the concept of expedition and these related words: *continental divide, headwaters, cartographer, treacherous, chronicling.*

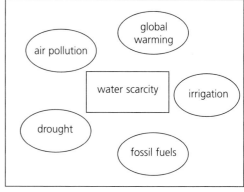

Concept Map

4. Have students place the concept in the middle oval and the related words on the lines above each oval.

5. Ask students to preview the text to learn more about these words. Students can read around boldface words.

6. Have pairs or small groups discuss their preview and use what they know to add details for each word listed on the Concept Map.

SET A PURPOSE FOR READING—Read to deepen your understanding of the concept and related words on your Concept Map.

AFTER READING AND DISCUSSING

- Have partners return to their Concept Maps to adjust details, add details to existing headings, or add another word that relates to the concept.

- Encourage partners or groups to share with classmates what they've learned and added to their vocabulary and Concept Maps. Then, ask the class to link the concept and related words to the topic.

> Here's what sixth graders said about "Drip Dry":
> *Water scarcity is what this [the article] is about. The related terms* fossil fuels *and* air pollution *relate to the topic because these lessen the water supply.*

> Here's what fifth graders said about "Lewis & Clark":
> *Expedition is what Lewis and Clark did.* Cartographer *and* chronicling *connect because they kept journals of the trip and what they saw and made maps. They crossed the* Continental Divide *and met up with* headwaters. *Treacherous is a word that tells what the expedition was like.*

FOLLOWING UP

- Continue having partners work on concepts and related vocabulary with other materials.

- Identify pairs that can work on this strategy independently.

- Find short bursts of time to support students who need an extra boost from you.

LESSON 5
Word Analysis Map

PURPOSE

To analyze a word from different perspectives and build students' knowledge of words; to ask small groups to become experts on a word and teach it to classmates

MATERIALS

"Drip Dry: Is It Possible That America's Water Sources Could One Day Be Tapped Out?" (pages 74–75); "Lewis & Clark: Journey Into the Unknown" (pages 76–78);

31

or any topic to be studied in science or social studies; a class set of the Word Analysis Map reproducible (page 82); four to six words preselected from the reading

TIME

10 minutes to complete map; 15 minutes for groups to present five to six words

PRESENTING THE LESSON

1. Introduce the strategy and explain how it enlarges students' knowledge of vocabulary related to the topic they're studying. Here's what I say:

   Word Analysis Maps are an effective way to study new words. Group members complete a map for one word, then teach one another. In this way, we can quickly introduce new and important words before reading. First, you write on your map the word and the parts of speech it can function as. Then you read around the word in the text and create a definition based on context clues. Group members discuss situations in which they think they could use this word and record these on the map. Next, groups discuss and list any features they know about this word and note some examples. One group member looks the word up in the dictionary and finds the definition that matches the way the word is used in the text. Group members discuss the definition, compare it to their explanation based on context clues, then write a sentence using one of the situations on their map.

   After reading and discussing, groups reconvene, discuss what they've learned about their word, adjust details on the map, and add new information.

2. Organize students into four to six small groups and give each group a copy of the Word Analysis Map.

3. Using a word from the reading material that students won't work on, show students how you complete the parts of the map. Here's what I write on the board or chart paper for *grueling* from "Lewis & Clark."

   Context Definition: exhausting, extremely tiring

   Part of Speech: adjective

   Situations: running a marathon; moving furniture into a house; taking a hard test

   Features: feeling worn out, putting forth lots of physical and mental effort

   Examples: training for a sport; carrying heavy furniture; fighting in a war; preparing for and taking a hard test

   Dictionary Definition: exhausting

   Sentence: I found lifting weights to prepare for the track meet a grueling experience. (adj.)

4. Give each group a word and a copy of the text they will read.

5. Have each group complete their maps using their assigned word.

6. Invite groups to share with classmates what they've learned about their word.

7. Display maps on a bulletin board so that students can reread one another's.

32

AFTER READING AND DISCUSSING

- Have groups return to their Word Analysis Maps to add and adjust ideas. Invite groups to present changes and additions to the class.

- Invite students to connect each word to the topic they're studying.

FOLLOWING UP

- Ask pairs to complete a Word Analysis Map once groups show they can successfully complete a map.

- Give each partner or group member a different word and a Word Analysis Map. Invite individuals to complete a map and share their findings with a partner or small group.

- Continue to model and use this strategy to build students' word and background knowledge before and after reading.

Name Jannelle   Date Mar. 2006

Title, Topic, and Pages Blizzard by Jim Murphy page 103
Word Analysis Map

Write the Word Here   Definition from Context
devastation   things broken, ripped
                                   destroyed

Part of Speech:
noun

List situations You Would Use The Word In Here:
after hurricane, a blizzard, tornado, bomb,
earthquake, fire, floods from rivers

What is it like? List any features here:
objects are broken, land is changed → makes a lake, floods,
beaches + trees destroyed, houses ruined, can't use items,
it's also widespread - the devastation

Give some related examples here:
houses burned by fire, no rain - drought ruin crops + hardens
land, insects eat crops

Write the Dictionary Definition that Explain the word used in the text:
ruin of property, waste

Choose one of the situations and use the word in a sentence:
Families felt shocked at the devastation caused
by the fire; for a block of homes were now piles
of charred rubble.

Sample Word Analysis Map

Continue to Think About . . .

As you prepare students to read about and study a topic in science or social studies, reflect on the benefits of enlarging the background and vocabulary knowledge of each student. The more you frontload students before reading about a new topic, the better they will comprehend and recall the new information. Before reading Chapter 3, take some time to reflect on these questions that focus on helping you think about the time you set aside to enlarge students' background knowledge:

- Why is it important to reserve time to build students' background knowledge of a topic before reading begins?

- Why do you decide to preteach vocabulary as part of the background knowledge students require to comprehend a topic?

- Why might you delay the study of a topic after investigating how much background knowledge students have?

CHAPTER 3

While Students Read

Self-Monitoring and Fix-Up Lessons That Improve Recall and Thinking

If you've had teaching experiences similar to mine, you've had students insist, "I read those pages, honest I did," even though they can't recall anything from the text. In fact, many were unaware that they weren't comprehending the material. Once you know that students are able to read the material and that they have sufficient background knowledge about the topic, then it's important to teach them strategies to monitor their understanding and recall as they read. Students also need fix-up strategies that allow them to repair the reading problem quickly, then continue to read and self-monitor (Garner, 1992; Gillet & Temple, 2000; Harvey & Goudvis, 2000; Robb, 2003; Vaughn & Estes, 1986).

Students can learn to self-monitor what they do and do not understand while reading, as long as the text is near their instructional level. If the text is too difficult for some students, you can find alternate materials on the same topic at a lower reading level; your school librarian can help you locate suitable material. Teaching students self-monitoring and fix-up strategies leads to independence with reading tasks and enables students to pinpoint reading problems and solve them immediately.

As You Read On . . .

In this chapter you will explore two self-monitoring strategies: the Sticky Note Strategy and Read/Pause/Retell/Evaluate. Following these metacognitive strategies are four fix-up strategies within two lessons: Reread, Close Read, Using Context Clues to Build Vocabulary, and Strategies for Pronouncing Words. This chapter has two parts. The first part introduces each strategy, then explains how it helps students pinpoint and repair reading difficulties. The second part contains brief, focused lessons that will help students apply the strategies while they read. Closing the chapter are some questions about self-monitoring for you to reflect on.

Self-Monitoring and Fix-Up Strategies

Whether students read science or social studies materials, they use the same self-monitoring and fix-up strategies. Explain to students that while they read, it's helpful to self-monitor by stopping after every two or three paragraphs, or after reading a section under a heading, to check whether they're understanding and remembering the text. If the text is challenging in parts, they should pause after two or three sentences or after each paragraph. Then they can return to reading longer sections of text.

Two Self-Monitoring Strategies: Lessons 6 and 7

When students monitor what they do and don't understand, they are in control of their reading and learning. The two self-monitoring strategies that follow—the Sticky Note Strategy and Read/Pause/Retell/Evaluate—enable students to identify parts of a text that confuse them. Once students can pinpoint challenging sections of the text, they can slow down and pause, then access a fix-up strategy such as Reread or Close Read. If it's a word that presents the comprehension challenge, students can try to use context clues to figure out its meaning, then continue to read.

DEVELOP STUDENTS' INDEPENDENCE

Once you demonstrate how to use the self-monitoring and fix-up strategies and ask students to apply them while they read materials, you'll find they will eventually absorb and own the strategies, developing the independence needed to read tough texts in and out of school.

6. Sticky Note Strategy: Introduction

Using sticky notes allows students to monitor their understanding of a text without writing on the text while they read. They can jot down a question and place the sticky note next to the part that confuses them. If it's a word that's difficult to understand, students jot down the word on a sticky note.

35

Each time students pinpoint parts of a text that they don't understand, they'll need to pause and access one of the fix-up strategies from Lessons 8 or 9. If the fix-up strategies don't help, students can return to their sticky notes after completing the reading and receive support from a peer partner or from you.

Sticky Note Strategy: *How It Helps Students Learn Content*

This strategy supports and improves students' comprehension and recall by:

- helping students identify passages and words that they don't understand
- having students pose a question about a passage that causes confusion or jot down a word that's not understood
- slowing down the reading and making it more thoughtful
- developing students' independence; students can self-monitor to discover what they do and do not understand and apply fix-up strategies as necessary.

7. Read/Pause/Retell/Evaluate: Introduction

This strategy asks students to pause after a chunk of difficult text and retell it in their own words. A chunk can be a sentence, several sentences, or a paragraph. Students check their retelling against the text; if they have recalled most of the details and can say key points in their own words, they are ready to continue reading. If not, it's time to apply a fix-up strategy.

Read/Pause/Retell/Evaluate: *How It Helps Students Learn Content*

This strategy supports and improves students' comprehension and recall by:

- asking them to pause frequently to check their recall and understanding while reading challenging texts or texts on unfamiliar topics
- asking them to ensure that they understand and recall new and unfamiliar details
- showing students how to check their retellings against the text
- having students apply fix-up strategies
- putting students in charge of their self-monitoring and asking them to decide the amount of text they need to read before pausing to retell and check, which leads to independence

Four Fix-Up Strategies: Lessons 8 and 9

Showing students how to use the fix-up strategies in this section provides them with tools for repairing derailed comprehension. Moreover, having fix-up tools that work enables students to solve their own reading problems, which will differ for each learner.

8. Reread or Close Read: Introduction

Here are two easy-to-apply fix-up strategies. Always ask students to reread a confusing passage first; encourage them to reread one to three times, bringing what they know and have learned about the topic to the challenging passage. Rereading often helps students make new connections to the text and helps them recall more details. If rereading doesn't support comprehension and recall, have students close read.

Close reading asks students to examine unfamiliar vocabulary, unclear pronoun references, or information that students aren't connecting to in order to increase comprehension. While close reading in science and social studies, students can also use nonfiction features related to the challenging passage to support understanding—features such as maps, charts, diagrams, sidebars, and photographs and captions.

Reread or Close Read: *How It Helps Students Learn Content*

Use Reread and Close Read to support and improve students' comprehension. These strategies help students understand passages and words that they don't understand by:

- helping them make clearer and stronger connections to tough passages
- untangling tricky pronoun references that can confuse
- focusing attention on facts and words that still confuse after rereading
- focusing attention on related nonfiction features to help students make connections to a passage

9. Using Context Clues to Build Vocabulary and Strategies for Pronouncing Words: Introduction

Two key strategies assist students when they bump into unfamiliar words in a text they're reading:

- using context clues embedded in the text to figure the meaning of a word
- learning ways to pronounce unfamiliar words

Writers often embed definitions or context clues in nonfiction texts or in the related text features such as charts and labels, diagrams, photographs and captions, and sidebars. They do this to help students figure out the meaning of a tough word and to provide clues that can help students pronounce new words. You can show students how to take apart a word, pronounce pieces they are familiar with (such as the prefix *dis-*), pronounce the parts, put them back together, then say the word. Quite often, students will recognize a word once they hear it said aloud; they might have heard it on the Internet or in a media presentation. Showing students how to use both strategies can equip them to handle the unfamiliar words they encounter in your units of study.

I've included a handout for students that lists the kinds of context clues authors give readers in nonfiction trade books and in textbooks (see page 84). Students can refer to this handout before reading, then seek help from a partner if they're stuck.

Using Context Clues to Build Vocabulary and Strategies for Pronouncing Words: *How It Helps Students Learn Content*

These strategies build students' vocabulary and improve comprehension and recall by:

- helping them deal with pronouncing and/or figuring out the meaning of unfamiliar words quickly and efficiently; research says that if students don't get a word in 30 seconds, they skip it.

- focusing attention on details in a text

Four Lessons That Move Students to Solving Problems While Reading

If students lack the strategies for dealing with unfamiliar words they meet in each new unit of study in science and social studies, then comprehension, recall, and word acquisition all suffer. The first two lessons that follow show you how to introduce two self-monitoring strategies that enable students to pinpoint what they do and don't understand: Sticky Note Strategy and Read/Pause/Retell/Evaluate. The last two lessons in this chapter include two fix-up strategies that improve comprehension and recall of information: Reread and Close Read—and two strategies that show students how to deal with unfamiliar words they don't understand and/or can't pronounce: Using Context Clues and Strategies for Pronouncing Words.

Sticky Note Strategy

PURPOSE

To help students identify confusing passages and unfamiliar words while they read

MATERIALS

"Drip Dry: Is It Possible That America's Water Sources Could One Day Be Tapped Out?" (pages 74–75); "Lewis & Clark: Journey Into the Unknown" (pages 76–78); or any short text on a topic to be studied in science or social studies; sticky notes for students

TIME

5 minutes to model for students

PRESENTING THE LESSON

1. Draw on chart paper two or three enlarged sticky notes that you can write on, as this way students can observe how you use the sticky note to self-monitor.

2. Name the strategy and explain how it can help your students. Here's what I say:

   Sticky notes can help you mark a place in a text you're reading, so you can ask a question about a part that confuses you or jot down an unfamiliar word. You can place the sticky note next to the confusing part so you can return to that part of the text if necessary. Before you continue to read, pause and try to resolve your confusion by applying a fix-up strategy.

   Sometimes it's a new word that can stump you and diminish understanding. Other times it can be several sentences, paragraphs, or an entire section that confuses you. Pause and apply a fix-up strategy (see Lessons 8 and 9 on pages 42–48). If none of these help, place a check on the sticky note; this is a signal to return to the word and/or section of text after reading and try to build your understanding. If you can't fix the problem on your own, try working with a partner.

   Today, I will read a section from an article and show you what I write on the sticky note I've drawn on chart paper. Listen carefully as I read aloud, then think-aloud, then write a question or word on the sticky note.

   THINK-ALOUD: **The section "Potent Pollution" in "Drip Dry"**
   [Pausing after reading the heading "Potent Pollution"] *I'm not sure what* potent *means. I'll write it on the sticky note along with the page it is on. Let me see if there*

> COMBINE SELF-MONITORING AND FIX-UP STRATEGY LESSONS
>
> *When you model a self-monitoring strategy, make sure you also teach students some fix-up strategies so that they have the tools to repair their understanding of confusing passages and tough words while they read.*

are clues in the text that can help me figure out the word's meaning. [Scans text.]
I learned that leaky underground gasoline tanks can cause cancer and that fertilizers from factories on the Mississippi River deprive fish of oxygen. Based on these facts, I think potent *means strong and dangerous.* [I jot these words on the sticky note.]

THINK-ALOUD: "Lewis & Clark"
[After reading aloud the title and also the subtitle, "A group of daring explorers headed west from Missouri nearly 200 years ago. Their journey would change the U.S. forever."]
I don't get how their journey could change our country forever. On the sticky note, I'll write, How can a journey change the U.S.? Now I'll read the first section. [Reads, stopping before "Starting Out."] *I still don't get it. I'll put a check on the sticky note and return to it after I complete the reading.* [Continues reading to the end.]
Now let me look at the map; it helps me understand that Lewis and Clark explored Jefferson's purchase—the Louisiana Territory. Their trip encouraged men and women to move further westward and develop the land. I think those are the changes.

4. Notice that I immediately accessed a fix-up strategy to try to address my confusion. If the strategy didn't work quickly, I would write a check on the sticky note, indicating that I needed to return to it to try to improve my understanding.

5. Give students sticky notes and ask them to use the strategy while they read an assigned section of your textbook or a trade book written at students' instructional levels.

AFTER READING AND DISCUSSING

- Have students who can support one another work in pairs.

- Help students who struggle to return to a sticky note and try to build comprehension.

- Have students check their sticky notes and return to those with checks to try to improve their understanding of a word, to pronounce a word, and/or to improve their understanding of a sentence or passage.

FOLLOWING UP

- Continue to have students use sticky notes with reading materials to monitor their understanding.

Read/Pause/Retell/Evaluate

PURPOSE

To model this self-monitoring strategy and show students how it helps pinpoint a passage that confuses

MATERIALS

"Drip Dry: Is It Possible That America's Water Sources Could One Day Be Tapped Out?" (pages 74–75); "Lewis & Clark: Journey Into the Unknown" (pages 76–78); or any short text on a topic to be studied in science or social studies; a class set of the Guidelines to Help You Close Read Tough Passages reproducible (page 83)

TIME

8 to 10 minutes

PRESENTING THE LESSON

1. Name the strategy and explain how it can help your students. Here's what I say:

    Adults and students both experience times while reading when the text doesn't make sense. The strategy Read/Pause/Retell/Evaluate helps you self-monitor your reading and determine what you do and don't understand. After you finish reading a long paragraph, a page, or a section in a textbook, you pause and retell what you've read without looking at the text. Then you check the text to make sure that your retelling included several important details. If you had difficulty retelling the passage in your own words, it means you're not comprehending fully, which is a sign to use a fix-up strategy such as Reread or Close Read to help you make sense of the reading (see Lesson 8 on pages 42–44).

2. Tell students that you will read aloud and retell a chunk of text. I model from "Drip Dry" and "Lewis & Clark," below.

    Here's what I do for "Drip Dry:"

    - First, I read the sidebar headed "Down and Out" to students.
    - Next, I retell: *A bad drought happened in the West in 1999. Reservoirs along the Colorado River dropped to half the normal level. That's all I recall.*
    - Now I check my recall against the text and evaluate my retelling. I note that I need to reread because there's lots more in the sidebar.
    - Here's what I add after rereading: *In seven states there were 25 million people who needed water. The drought led to people saving water by changing to water-saving toilets and washing machines. In Denver, the rate at which people now consume water is the lowest in 30 years.* I evaluate again by checking with the text and note that I can read on. If I could not recall many details, I would reread slowly, bringing what I know about diminishing water supplies to the text.

Here's what I do for "Lewis & Clark":

- First, I read aloud the section under "Chronicling the West."

- Next, I retell: *The group saw amazing sights like the White Cliffs that are in Montana. Lewis kept journals; others kept journals, too. They wrote what they saw—they wrote in great detail. These journals were valuable because it gave others a sense of the land features and the animals encountered.*

- Now I check my retelling against the text. I see that I did remember the important details, so I can read on.

3. Notice how I evaluated my retelling, which enabled me to decide whether to read on, reread, or close read. I explain to students that the ability to evaluate their recall of details can truly help them enlarge their knowledge about a topic and use this to improve their comprehension.

CHOOSING A FIX-UP STRATEGY

Here are some questions that can help you evaluate your retellings, then choose a fix-up strategy:

- *Do I need to slow down and reread?*

- *Are there strong images that can help me visualize?*

- *Did a word stump me? If so, should I read on or use context clues?*

- *Should I close read and try to connect ideas to what I read before?*

AFTER READING AND DISCUSSING

- Organize students into pairs and encourage partners to discuss Read/Pause/Retell/Evaluate and whether it helped them with comprehension.

FOLLOWING UP

- Continue having students apply this self-monitoring strategy to challenging sections of text.

- Have pairs who can work independently complete the strategy together. Both read a section. Partners take turns retelling different sections and checking to evaluate whether the retelling included enough details.

- Practice with students who struggle and help them move to independence.

LESSON 8

Reread or Close Read

PURPOSE

To show students how the fix-up strategies, Reread and Close Read, can repair their recall and comprehension

MATERIALS

"Drip Dry: Is It Possible That America's Water Sources Could One Day Be Tapped Out?" (pages 74–75); "Lewis & Clark: Journey Into the Unknown" (pages 76–78);

or any short text on a topic to be studied in science or social studies; a class set of the Guidelines to Help You Close Read Tough Passages reproducible (page 83)

TIME

5 to 8 minutes for each lesson

PRESENTING THE LESSON FOR REREADING

1. Name the strategy and explain how it can help your students. Here's what I say:

   Rereading the part of a text that confuses you is an effective way to improve your understanding and recall. If you had difficulty retelling a paragraph or section of text and recalling specific details, it means that you're not comprehending; this is a sign to access a fix-up strategy to help you make sense of the text. Today, I'll introduce a fix-up strategy called Reread. With this strategy, you slowly reread the passage, trying to connect what you know about the topic to the author's words. Then, retell to check your recall. If you still have difficulty retelling specific details after the second rereading, ask a partner or me for help.

2. Read aloud a short selection; you may choose to use the selection at the right from "Drip Dry" or the other on page 44 from "Lewis & Clark."

   Tell students that you will retell what you've read without looking at the paragraph, then evaluate the retelling to determine whether you recall enough details to continue reading, or if you need to slow down and reread.

   ### RETELLINGS FOR "DRIP DRY":
   Here's my first retelling.

   A man named Gleick says there's two reasons for short water supplies. The first is that more than 95 percent of Earth's water is saltwater. We can't drink saltwater. Removing the salt is extremely expensive.

   I evaluate my retelling and note I only remembered one reason. I reread the passage and try to recall the second reason. Here's my second retelling:

   A lot of our freshwater supplies can't be used—like glaciers. Some of the water supply isn't spread evenly among states—an example is that Arizona is dry and the Great Lakes generally just supply states that border them with freshwater. Now I can continue to read.

   ### RETELLINGS FOR THE PASSAGE FROM "LEWIS & CLARK":
   Here's my first retelling.

   Clark made maps for the group. Another name for mapmaker is cartographer. Clark made maps of the mountains, rivers, and the land.

EXCERPT FROM "DRIP DRY" BY SEAN PRICE

How could a liquid that covers two thirds of Earth be in short supply? There are two main reasons, says Peter Gleick, a water expert at the research group Pacific Institute: First, 97 percent of the world's water is saltwater— useless for drinking or nurturing crops unless expensive desalination techniques are used to purify it. Second, much of the remaining freshwater is either in an unusable form, like glaciers, or unevenly distributed due to geography and climate (average weather in an area over time.) "The fact that there's a lot of water in the Great Lakes doesn't help people in Arizona," Gleick says.

43

I evaluate my retelling, and decide that I need to reread the passage again. Here's my second retelling:

*Clark made maps for the group. Another name for mapmaker
is cartographer. Clark made maps of the mountains, rivers, and
the land. Lewis identified 178 plants and 122 animals—all were
new to scientists. The coyote and porcupine were two of these
new animals. Now I can continue to read.*

3. Model two or three more times on different days so that students can observe the power of rereading slowly as an aid to recall and understanding.

4. Point out that you paraphrase the details in your retellings; you put them into your own words to show that you understand the information.

FOLLOWING UP

- Remind students to apply this strategy when they are reading texts in which they have a small amount of background knowledge or in which the writing is difficult, thereby making unpacking meaning tough.

- Encourage students to paraphrase.

PRESENTING THE LESSON FOR CLOSE READ

1. Name the strategy and explain how it can help your students. Here's what I say:

    *Close Read is a helpful fix-up strategy because it asks you to put the
    confusing text under a microscope and go through it word by word
    and phrase by phrase and bring what you know to the text to
    construct meaning and connect ideas among words and phrases.*

2. Pass out the student handout with guidelines for Close Read (see page 83). These guidelines will refresh students' memories of the fix-up strategy and support them when they use it independently.

3. Have students read their handout and ask clarifying questions.

4. Explain to students that Close Read can help them read the text with improved understanding because they zoom in on and examine tricky words and phrases.

5. Read aloud one of the selections on page 45: One is from "Drip Dry" and the other is from "Lewis & Clark." Model doing a Close Read.

    CLOSE READ FOR THE PASSAGE FROM "DRIP DRY":

    *I understand that automobiles make nitrogen oxide that pollutes the air and causes
    acid rain. It's unclear if the autos make sulfur dioxide. But I do know that sulfur dioxide
    is a fossil fuel pollutant that comes either from coal or oil; the first sentence says that.*

44

Acid rain hurts plants and fish, which are part of the food chain. Even though the passage didn't say this, I can infer that acid rain can also get into wells and spoil drinking water.

Note how I had to infer and use information to figure out the origin of the pollutant sulfur dioxide. Sometimes, even a Close Read doesn't clear up all the questions I have. Class discussions and research on the Internet can help.

CLOSE READ FOR THE PASSAGE FROM "LEWIS & CLARK":

The map on page 77 helped me see the Rocky Mountains. I'm not sure what watershed *means and there are no clues here. I looked up the term* Continental Divide *in the dictionary, and it says that the mountains divide or separate rivers that flow into the Atlantic Ocean from rivers that flow into the Pacific Ocean. Then I looked up* watershed *in the dictionary and found that it is the area drained by a river. The mountains separate the rivers and their watersheds on the west side from those on the east side.*

> EXCERPT FROM "DRIP DRY" BY SEAN PRICE
>
> *Burning fossil fuels, such as coal and oil, emits air pollutants. U.S. autos produce 8.2 million tons of nitrogen oxide a year. This, along with sulfur dioxide and other pollutants, makes acid rain. Precipitation—rain, snow, hail, or sleet—mixes with the poisons and slowly kills plants and fish.*

> EXCERPT FROM "LEWIS & CLARK" BY MATT WARSHAUER
>
> *Continental Divide: a series of mountain ridges extending from Alaska to Mexico that form the watershed of North America.*

6. Note that when definitions in texts are unclear, I turned to the dictionary. You could also use a glossary if your book contains one.

FOLLOWING UP

- Frequently remind students that if rereading twice doesn't improve recall and comprehension of a tough passage, then they should Close Read to try to improve their understanding.

- Ask students to use their handout to remind them of the elements of close reading.

LESSON 9
Using Context Clues to Build Vocabulary and Strategies for Pronouncing Words

PURPOSE

To figure out the meanings of unfamiliar words using context clues; to provide strategies for pronouncing unfamiliar words

MATERIALS

"Drip Dry: Is It Possible That America's Water Sources Could One Day Be Tapped

Out?" (pages 74–75); "Lewis & Clark: Journey Into the Unknown" (pages 76–78); or a short text on any topic to be studied in science or social studies; a class set of the Context Clues reproducible (page 84)

TIME

5 minutes for each lesson

PRESENTING THE LESSON ON USING CONTEXT CLUES TO BUILD VOCABULARY

1. Organize students into pairs.

2. Name the strategy and explain how it can help your students. Here's what I say:

   Using Context Clues can help you figure out the meanings of many of the new words you meet in science (or social studies). At times, just rereading the sentence can help you figure out the word's meaning. If that doesn't work, read the sentence before and after the one with the tough word, looking for clues. In textbooks and nonfiction, writers sometimes include a definition of the word or say it in another way immediately after the word. When you spot a comma or parentheses after a word, that's a clue that a definition is close by. Other times, you can figure out the definitions by using details in the paragraph the word is part of. Remember to search for meaning clues in nonfiction features such as sidebars, photographs and captions, and diagrams. Knowing the kinds of clues to look for can help you figure out a word's meaning quickly.

3. Distribute the handout on different kinds of context clues on page 84.

4. Model how to use context clues using a sample sentence from your recent reading.

   In science, I write this sentence from "Drip Dry" on the board:
   *Robbi Savage, president of World Water Monitoring Day, says some of the most **pervasive** pollution now comes from household chemicals such as oil and pesticides.*

   I point out that this sentence contains a concrete example that helps me figure out the meaning of *pervasive*. The example is "household chemicals such as oil and pesticides." The word *household* lets the reader know these pollutants are in every household, so there's tons of them. So *pervasive* means everywhere—in all households in our country.

   In social studies, I write this sentence from "Lewis & Clark" on the board: *We shall **delineate** [mark] with correctness the great arteries [rivers] of this great country.*

   I read the sentence aloud and point out that the definition is in brackets that come right after the word. I explain that many textbooks use this kind of context clue, and I note that often a comma comes after a challenging word and may signal an upcoming definition.

5. Ask students to complete an assigned reading in class or at home and jot down an unfamiliar word and the page it appears on, as well as the type of context clue. Students can share their findings with a partner, a small group, or the entire class.

46

FOLLOWING UP

- Continue to review the kinds of context clues on the handout by encouraging students to point to and share with the class a specific type they come across in their reading.

- Keep asking students to find examples to share for the different categories on the handout.

- Refer to the box below that provides you with strategies to share with students that give them options if context clues aren't enough.

SHOW STUDENTS HOW TO USE THE DICTIONARY

Modeling how to use the dictionary effectively is crucial because students tend to choose the first or shortest definition, without considering whether it relates to the meaning of the text.

What to Do When Context Clues Aren't Enough

Sometimes there are insufficient context clues in your text, or none at all. What follows are some ideas for preteaching key words that are not surrounded by adequate context clues.

- Compose a sentence with strong context clues and write it on the chalkboard. Ask students to figure out the word's meaning.

- Compose a web that includes what students already know about the word and lead a discussion of the word.

- Ask students to jot down tough words on a sticky note or in their journal, noting the title of the book and the page number of the word that stumped them. Students or partners reading the same text can look up the word in the dictionary. Remind students to search for the meaning in the dictionary that matches the meaning in the text.

PRESENTING THE LESSON ON STRATEGIES FOR PRONOUNCING WORDS

1. Name the strategy and explain how it can help your students. Here's what I say:

   Besides using context clues, there's another strategy that can help you figure out a new word: hearing it said aloud. There are several ways to figure out how to pronounce a word that is unfamiliar. The point is to avoid guessing, because that can change the sentence's meaning. Reread the word, looking carefully at the beginning, middle, and end of it. Remove and say prefixes and suffixes. Try to say the root or base word, then put all the parts together. If there are no word parts that you recognize, try breaking the word into syllables. Pronounce each one, then put the sounds together. Let's try this together.

2. Organize students into pairs.

3. Give students words with prefixes and suffixes for practice. I write these on the board: *outstripping, thermoelectric, intentions, desalination*

Have pairs work through the process using the second strategy, Guidelines for Using Clues in the Word, then share what they've done with classmates.

Guidelines for Pronouncing Words

- Look closely at the beginning, middle, and end of the word.
  Example: *precipitation* from "Drip Dry"
- If the word has a prefix, try to say it, then take it off. (*pre-*)
- If the word has a suffix, try to say it, then take it off. (*-tion*)
- Look at the base or root word that's left. Try saying the base word and blending all the word parts together.
- Reread the sentence. See whether the word makes sense and whether you understand what it means.

FOLLOWING UP

- Choose words that will challenge students and have them work with a partner to try to pronounce the word and figure out its meaning.

Continue to Think About . . .

Most of the time we teachers focus on building comprehension and vocabulary after reading. This chapter shows you how you can provide students with strategies that enable them to handle meaning and vocabulary problems *while* reading. With these strategies, students can build word knowledge and improve comprehension as they read. Use the questions that follow to reflect on what you are doing to move students to independence with solving reading problems—problems that if left unsolved can diminish comprehension and recall.

- How many times have I modeled how to self-monitor reading and how it can improve understanding? How can this help students?

- Do I remind students to self-monitor? How frequently do I offer them opportunities to discuss their self-monitoring with a partner?

- How often am I modeling fix-up strategies to show students how they can repair reading problems? Why is this important?

- Have I given students both handouts for word building and walked them through each one? How can these handouts support students?

- How many times a week do I spend 5 to 10 minutes supporting students who need more explicit modeling from me? Why is this important?

48

CHAPTER 4

After Students Read

Six Lessons That Teach Students to Analyze and Synthesize

After-learning experiences are ideal opportunities for asking students to
reflect on, think about, and apply what they've learned. Moreover, providing
experiences that ask them to process new information and build new
understandings is vital if they are to move beyond memorizing a discrete set
of facts. Vaughn and Estes (1986) call these opportunities "contemplation" or
"reasoned reflections that enable understandings to be synthesized" (page
156). However, to discuss, think, and write to learn and analyze
information, students require time in class to mull over ideas and make
meaningful connections, do some research, talk to peers, and surf the
Internet (Alvermann & Phelps, 1998; Keene & Zimmermann, 1997; Robb,
2003, 2007; Tierney & Readence, 2000; Vacca & Vacca, 2000).

Time spent writing, taking notes, reviewing material collaboratively,
and writing short summaries enables students to enlarge their knowledge
of a topic and construct new understanding. All of these after-reading
experiences are easy to model. I've selected activities that students can
grasp quickly and that are practical and will support their comprehension,
recall, and ability to make connections to other ideas and texts.

*Lesson 11, Think With
Heading Notes, and
Lesson 12, Question/Answer/
Connect/React, invite
students to start the note-
taking process before they
read. So in Lesson 11,
students use headings in
texts to set purposes for
reading. In Lesson 12,
students pose questions
using nonfiction features
before reading. Both setting
purposes and posing
questions create a
framework for reading
and discussing material
and for taking notes. **The
writing of the notes and
thinking with them
occurs after reading.***

Each activity can become an assessment that demonstrates what students do and don't understand. These assessments can be graded so that you have marks in addition to the traditional tests and quizzes. The important point to remember is to tell students when these activities are for practice and when you will grade them. Knowing this is not only fair to students, but allows them to put additional effort into their work. For each activity, the reproducible's instructions contain the criteria for your expectations. You can use these criteria to respond to students' work and to assign a grade.

As You Read On . . .

I've divided the chapter into two parts. The first part introduces six after-reading lessons that build vocabulary, as well as teach students how to take notes, review and study for a test, write a short summary, and develop a hypothesis, then support it. For each lesson, you'll find an introduction followed by a section that explains how the strategy helps students learn content.

The second part of this chapter contains six brief lessons that you can adapt to the population you teach. I've included reproducibles in the appendix that go with each activity in this section. You'll also find a student handout in the appendix on taking notes, with tips that can refresh students' memories of your modeling and expectations. Before you move on to the last chapter, you'll find several questions that invite you to reflect on offering students after-reading activities.

Six After-Reading and Discussing Activities

These activities can enlarge students' vocabulary and their recall of the information you consider important. In addition, students will learn how to take notes, then reflect on why the information is important.

I've placed note taking in the after-reading section so that students have had a chance to reflect on the material, make some connections, and can write notes in their own words. For students to determine the important ideas in a reading selection, they must have clear purposes for reading and thinking because it's the purposes that enable students to select important details and ideas.

You'll find three different note-taking strategies, each of which asks students to think deeply about their reading. Introduce the strategies one at a time and give students several weeks of practice with one before moving to another. With three note-taking strategies under their belts, students can choose the one they enjoy most or choose the activity that best meets the demands of the text.

10. Word Map: Introduction

Creating a Word Map is a top-notch after-learning strategy because it shows students how much they have learned about key words from a unit of study and indicates whether they need to review terms before taking a test or quiz. There are four parts to the Word Map (see reproducible on page 85).

■ The first part asks, "What is it?" and invites students to write the word and a synonym or similar word.

■ The second part asks, "What is it like?" Here, students note the features and characteristics of the word.

■ The third part asks students to give some examples of the word.

■ The fourth part asks students to use the word in a sentence that shows their understanding of the word.

Organize students into pairs so they can discuss the four elements before completing their maps.

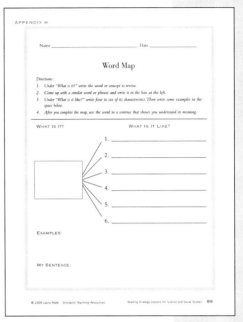

Word Map

Word Map: How It Helps Students Enlarge Their Vocabulary

This activity supports recall and understanding by:

■ asking students to list all the features and/or characteristics of the word

■ having students provide examples of the word

■ informing students whether they have understood an important word or term

■ having students use the word in a sentence that showcases their knowledge of it

11. Think With Heading Notes: Introduction

This framework for note taking is simple: The boldface headings in students' textbooks become the main headings for each section of notes. Students copy the boldface headings from their text and use these as their purposes for reading to figure out key details. Students write notes in a bulleted list under each heading in their own words. After taking notes, students reread one section at a time and make connections and inferences by asking: *How do these details relate to the topic? Why is this information important? How does it affect people?*

STUDENT HANDOUT ON NOTE TAKING

Before you introduce the strategies on taking notes in Lessons 11, 12, and 13, make sure you give each student a copy of the handout on page 86 and review it with them. Students can keep the handout in their notebooks and refer to the tips each time they take notes. If you have time, organize students into pairs and have them share and discuss their notes, then add any additional thoughts that surfaced. Doing this supports recall and understanding of the material.

Think With Heading Notes: *How It Helps Students Determine Important Ideas and Think With Them*

The activity supports students' taking notes and thinking with them by:

- guiding students to use headings and reading purposes to determine key ideas
- having students write notes in their own words to show that they understand the material
- having students think about what their notes mean and why they are important
- encouraging students to return to the text after reading to develop a deeper understanding of the material

12. Question/Answer/Connect/React: Introduction

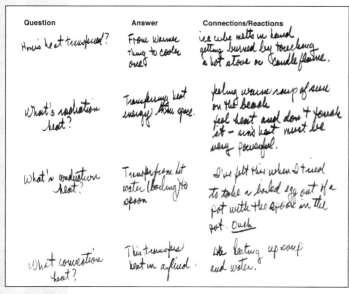

Sample notes for Question/Answer/Connect/React

Students use boldface headings, vocabulary words, photographs and captions, diagrams, and graphs to pose questions *before reading*; their questions become *purposes for reading* and discovering answers. After reading, students answer their questions in their own words; these become part of their notes. Then students reread their notes and write their reactions to them, or make a connection to another text, to a movie, or to something seen on the Internet. Students can also make connections to how the information can change lives or help people, animals, or the environment. A reproducible on page 87 helps guide them through this process.

Question/Answer/Connect/React: *How It Helps Students Think and Analyze*

This activity supports note taking and thinking about notes by:

- having students use questions as purposes for reading and thinking about text
- asking students to write, in their own words, answers to their questions
- having students reread their notes, then make connections and/or write their reactions

13. The 5 W's: Taking Notes and Writing Summaries: Introduction

The 5 W's are who, what, when, where, and why. They can be used as a framework for selecting important details from a passage (see page 88 for student organizer). After students read and discuss a chapter or selection, they can use each W to help them identify important information to jot down. You can have students use the 5 W's Organizer solely for taking notes, or at times you can ask them to transform these notes into a short summary (see sidebar for an explanation of each W). For a summary, have students write a title and a topic sentence that announces the subject, then take the details they noted under each W and create one or two sentences for each.

The 5 W's Framework: Taking Notes and Writing Summaries: *How It Helps Students Determine Important Ideas*

Using this organizer helps students take notes, think about the information, and summarize it by:

- providing a clear framework for selecting and organizing important details

- asking them to explain *why* so they can make connections and broaden their thinking about the topic

AN EXPLANATION OF EACH W

Write these on chart paper and discuss with students before giving them the organizer on page 88 to complete. You can use these to think aloud and model how you take notes for each W.

- *Who (or what) is this about?*
- *What happened?*
- *When did it happen?*
- *Where did it happen?*
- *Why did it happen?*
- *Why is it significant? (Consider connections to self, other texts, technology, and community and world issues.)*

14. Collaborative Review Sheet: Introduction

This activity places the responsibility of reviewing for a test on students. Three to four days before you plan on giving a test, organize students into groups of four or five. Give each student a copy of the review sheet on page 89. Take 15 minutes from each class period and have students complete the chapter/unit review on separate paper. Point out the section that asks students to budget and plan their study time at home. Make suggestions the first two or three times you review this way, then invite students to plan their study time independently.

Photocopy the questions each group feels will be on the test, for these will support their studying. You can also use some of students' questions on the test.

Make sure you take notes on questions students have about the topic and review this material prior to the test.

Collaborative Review Sheet: *How It Helps Students Prepare for Tests*

This activity supports reviewing and studying for tests by:

- engaging students in the process of reviewing material and studying it

- having students collaborate, so they can support one another

- inviting students to predict important information they should learn

- challenging students to create questions that they believe will be on the test

15. Forming a Hypothesis and Supporting It: Introduction

Once students have completed a unit of study, you can ask them to form a hypothesis or develop an opinion about the information presented and take notes using the organizer

53

on page 90. To start the process, teach students what a hypothesis or an opinion statement is and how to form one. Next, you'll need to show students how to select details and facts from the text to support the hypothesis or opinion. Finally, you'll ask students to evaluate their position based on the amount of support they found in the text.

Students can use their notes to plan a short paragraph (see Plan Your Opinion Paragraph on page 91). Their hypothesis becomes a topic sentence and their notes become the support for their position. Students will need to add a title.

Forming a Hypothesis and Supporting It: *How It Helps Students Defend a Position*
This thinking activity helps students by:

- asking them to evaluate information in their text and develop a hypothesis about it

- having them analyze details and select relevant ones

- inviting students to skim and/or reread parts of the text in order to gather support for their hypothesis

- inviting students to analyze their data and turn their analysis into a writing plan

- having students turn a plan into a paragraph that supports their hypothesis

Six Lessons That Improve Recall and Encourage Thinking With Information

The six lessons that follow encourage reflection and help students use information studied and learned to think, make connections, build new background knowledge and understandings, and enrich their vocabulary. Because discussions and writing are an integral part of each activity, students will quickly be able to pinpoint information that they understand and details that still confuse them. This is the ideal time in a unit of study to review, reteach, or find peer support for those who require extra modeling.

LESSON 10

Word Map

PURPOSE

To offer an opportunity for students to show what they know and recall about a concept and/or key word

MATERIALS

"Drip Dry: Is It Possible That America's Water Sources Could One Day Be Tapped Out?" (pages 74–75); "Lewis & Clark: Journey Into the Unknown" (pages 76–78); or a short text on any topic to be studied in science or social studies; a class set of the Word Map reproducible (page 85)

TIME

5 to 8 minutes to model; 10 to 12 minutes for students to complete a Word Map

PRESENTING THE LESSON

1. Name the activity and explain how it helps students think about key vocabulary and concepts. Here's what I say:

   Completing this activity asks you to reflect on an important word or concept we've studied. Once you can list all the characteristics of the word, give examples, and use the word in a sentence, you'll know that you have deepened your understanding and have absorbed enough information to use that word.

2. Show students how you complete a word map for a key term. Here's what I model for students. Write your thinking on chart paper or the board.

MODEL MAP: "Drip Dry" by Sean Price

What is it? **drought**. *Another word or phrase:* **lack of water**

What is it like?

- short or no water supply
- scarcity of water supplies
- little or no rain
- land dries and cracks
- plants die
- pollutants cause it

Examples:

- low reservoirs
- limited home use
- lower all consumption
- water rationing

Sentence: The summer **drought** *dried up the corn that we planted.*

MODEL MAP: "Lewis & Clark" by Matt Warshauer

What is it? **expedition**. *Another word or phrase:* **journey**

What is it like?

- voyage
- exploration
- exploring the unknown
- uses men and machines
- dangerous
- gather data

Examples:

- rockets
- space shuttle
- astronauts
- explorers

Sentence: Preparations for the **expedition** *to the North Pole took three months.*

---

3. Organize students into pairs.

4. Give each student a copy of the Word Map reproducible on page 85.

5. Give each pair a word or concept and have them discuss what they know about it, then complete the word map.

6. Have students share with their classmates what they know about the word/concept.

7. Ask students to add to their word maps any new information learned.

FOLLOWING UP

• Continue having pairs work together to complete Word Maps as a closing activity for a unit of study.

• Set aside time for partners to share their maps with the entire class.

• Divide a list of several important words among partners or small groups, asking them to complete a map for one word. Then, have pairs or groups share with the class as a review.

LESSON 11

Think With Heading Notes

PURPOSE

To help students write notes in their own words and use these to think about, connect to, and analyze the information

MATERIALS

"Drip Dry: Is It Possible That America's Water Sources Could One Day Be Tapped Out?" (pages 74–75); "Lewis & Clark: Journey Into the Unknown" (pages 76–78); or a short text on any topic to be studied in science or social studies

TIME

5 to 8 minutes

For Lessons 11 to 13, give students the handout on page 86. They can use this for all kinds of note-taking.

PRESENTING THE LESSON

1. Name the activity and explain how it helps students determine important details, then figure out what this information means and why it's important. Here's what I say:

This activity invites you to take notes after reading, then think about the information you've learned. You will be able to select important details by using your purposes for reading along with the headings for each section of text. In addition to taking notes in your own words to show that you understand the material, you'll reread the notes for each heading and explain what the information means and why it's important. In this way, taking notes moves beyond jotting down the facts to using the facts to think about the topic and determine the relevance of specific details and ideas.

2. Demonstrate how you create heading notes.

HEADING NOTES: "DRIP DRY":

Here are the important facts/notes I share for "Water World" from "Drip Dry."

Water World

- *saltwater on earth—97%*
- *saltwater—can't drink it, can't water crops with it*
- *desalination—takes salt out—too expensive*
- *some of the freshwater is in glaciers and can't be used*
- *freshwater is not in the same amounts in all parts of the U.S.A.*
- *population keeps growing rapidly—we won't have enough freshwater by 2080*

Next, I pose two questions that push students to thinking with these notes: *What does this information mean? Why is this information important?*

Here are the responses to these questions that I share with students.

What does this information mean? *This means that freshwater supplies are limited on Earth. As the number of people grows, having enough water for them is a big problem.*

Why is this information important? *It's important to know this so we can find ways to increase the freshwater supply and have enough by 2080.*

HEADING NOTES: "LEWIS & CLARK":

Here are the important facts/notes I share for "Chronicling the West" from "Lewis & Clark."

Chronicling the West

- *the Corps saw amazing sights on their journey*
- *Lewis noted that the White Cliffs in what is today Montana were remarkable*
- *Lewis and others wrote what they saw in journals*

Now I show students how I think with these notes by using the questions that follow.

What does this information mean? *Lewis and others took the time to document what they saw in the new territory. It showed that they took their exploration seriously and wanted to keep careful records of the journey.*

Why is this information important? *Several Corps members wrote about the wonders they saw, which gives historians different perspectives of the land. It also served to explain to those not on the journey exactly what the men saw and experienced.*

---

3. Ask students to complete heading notes on their own, then reread the notes for each section.

4. Have students complete the thinking part after each section, using the questions: *What does this information mean? Why is this information important?*

FOLLOWING UP

- Have students complete heading notes several times so they absorb the process.

- Make sure students reread each section and explain what it means and why the information is important.

LESSON 12

Question/Answer/Connect/React

PURPOSE

To show students that questions and answers can become a note-taking framework

MATERIALS

"Drip Dry: Is It Possible That America's Water Sources Could One Day Be Tapped Out?" (pages 74–75); "Lewis & Clark: Journey Into the Unknown" (pages 76–78); or a short text on any topic to be studied in science or social studies; a class set of the Question/Answer/Connect/React reproducible (page 87)

TIME

7 to 10 minutes

PRESENTING THE LESSON

1. Name the activity and explain how it helps students use questions to drive their reading and use their answers as notes. Afterward, students form connections and reactions to their notes, which strengthens their comprehension. Here's what I say:

This activity asks you to create questions before reading, based on your preview of nonfiction features in the text, such as boldface headings, vocabulary, photographs and captions, sidebars, diagrams, charts, and maps. These questions become your purposes for reading the selection. Having the questions helps you figure out the important details while you read. After reading, you can skim the text to find

58

Reading Strategy Lessons for Science & Social Studies

answers to your questions, then jot them down. Next, you'll reread each query and your response, then make connections to other topics, information on the Internet, movies, magazine articles, and videos. You can also make connections to why you think the information is important and how it can change lives. This kind of thinking will enrich your understanding of the text.

2. Model the process. Here's what I write on chart paper (or the board) for "Drip Dry" and "Lewis and Clark." I prefer using chart paper, so students have a resource to refer to when they are completing work on their own.

SAMPLE RESPONSE: "Drip Dry" by Sean Price

QUESTION	ANSWER	CONNECTION/REACTION
Why won't there be enough freshwater in the future?	*Population will double by 2080, but freshwater is diminishing due to pollution, droughts, and waste.*	*We need to do more research on ways to save water in homes and factories. We need to make people aware of these problems so that everyone will help. This could be a dangerous situation unless we do research and change our ways*

SAMPLE RESPONSE: "Lewis & Clark" by Matt Warshauer

QUESTION	ANSWER	CONNECTION/REACTION
Who was the "Great Father"?	*Jefferson told Lewis and Clark to make friends with the Indian tribes. Lewis and Clark studied about 50 tribes. They told the tribes that Jefferson was their new "Great Father." The tribes were now part of the U.S.*	*This, to me, was a takeover of large groups of people and their land without any choice for the Indian tribes and with no payment. The Indians helped the Corps all along and made the journey of Lewis and Clark a success. My feeling is that the Indian nations did not have a fair deal.*

3. Give students a copy of the reproducible on page 87 or help them set up their journals with the headings in the sample above.

4. Invite students to practice using material they are studying in your class.

FOLLOWING UP

- Continue providing opportunities for students to practice this framework.
- Make sure students complete the Connections/Reactions part; this is where they can think with the facts.

The 5 W's: Taking Notes and Writing Summaries

PURPOSE

To show students how to collect important details using this framework; to turn the 5 W's notes into a short summary

MATERIALS

"Drip Dry: Is It Possible That America's Water Sources Could One Day Be Tapped Out?" (pages 74–75); "Lewis & Clark: Journey Into the Unknown" (pages 76–78); or a short text on any topic to be studied in science or social studies; a class set of the 5 W's Organizer reproducible (page 88)

TIME

10 minutes for note taking; 10 minutes for writing a summary

PRESENTING THE LESSON

1. Name the activity and explain how it helps students take notes, make connections, and develop a framework for writing summaries. Here's what I say:

   This activity invites you to take notes by using a framework we call the 5 W's Organizer, which guides you to record information in the following categories: who or what it's about, what, when, where, and why. Once you've read and discussed a chapter in your textbook or another nonfiction text, use what you've learned to complete the 5 W's Organizer. It's important to take detailed and specific notes in your own words, which means you might have to skim or reread parts of a text. Your 5 W's notes can help you write complete identifications on tests or for homework about a person, event, concept, new word, or idea. These notes can also help you write a summary of the text. First you come up with a title and topic sentence; then you transform the information under each of the W's into sentences that support your topic sentence. We'll go over all this together.

2. Give each student a 5 W's Organizer (see page 88).

3. Review the explanation of each W, pointing out that *who* refers to a person and *what* to an event or concept.

4. Here are completed organizers that I share with students.

USING "DRIP DRY" BY SEAN PRICE

WHO OR WHAT: *Drought and short freshwater supplies*

WHAT: *In the U.S., carefree use of freshwater needs to change. Population is growing, more people need water, less water to go around.*

WHEN: *This is happening now; by 2080 the U.S. population will double. There's not enough water now—there will be less in the future.*

WHERE: *In the U.S. and all over the world; it's a global problem.*

WHY: *In the U.S. drought—lack of rain—has caused reservoirs to go down; using ice in drinks, watering lawns in places like Arizona that have less rain, use precious water. Pollution by chemicals from factories, by burning fossil fuels, and by global warming will all reduce our water supplies. We need to work to make better appliances that use less water, find alternate fuels, and not allow companies to pollute rivers. Otherwise, there will not be enough water for future generations.*

USING "LEWIS & CLARK" BY MATT WARSHAUER

WHO OR WHAT: *Lewis and Clark*

WHAT: *Sent on an expedition with a Corps of men to explore the Louisiana Territory and Oregon Country. Told by President Jefferson to make friends with the Indian nations. Almost 50 tribes that Lewis and Clark met were told they were now part of the U.S. and that President Jefferson was their new "Great Father."*

WHEN: *May 14, 1804, to September 23, 1806*

WHERE: *Unexplored Louisiana Territory and Oregon Country*

WHY: *The explorations of Lewis & Clark mapped out this unexplored land for future generations. Their maps and journals led to westward expansion because they described a land rich with natural wonders, animals, and other resources. The Corps depended on Native Americans to guide them through this unknown territory. Sacagawea, a Shoshone, showed the group where to cross the Rocky Mountains and how to find roots and vegetables they could eat. Sacagawea led the way for other tribes to accept the strangers. The reaction and connection I have is that the U.S. took the land from Native American tribes who helped the explorers build canoes for the last part of the journey, but did not pay them or help them understand what was happening. This changed the future of American and Native American relationships.*

---

5. Have students complete their 5 W's Organizer. Explain that the *why* is important because it asks them to think and to make connections with and react to the details.

ON ANOTHER DAY

1. Explain to students that they can use their 5 W's notes to write a summary.

2. Have students reread their notes, then create a title and a sentence that introduces the topic in an interesting way. Here's what I share with students.

> TITLE AND TOPIC SENTENCE: "Drip Dry"
>
> TITLE: *Deadly Drought*
>
> TOPIC SENTENCE: *By 2080, the number of people living in the U.S. will double, while our freshwater supply continues to diminish.*

> TITLE AND TOPIC SENTENCE: "Lewis & Clark"
>
> TITLE: *New Frontiers*
>
> TOPIC SENTENCE: *Jefferson's Louisiana Purchase and the explorations of Lewis and Clark doubled the size of the U.S. and opened the West for Americans.*

3. Now, have students turn each W into one or a few sentences.

4. Ask them to wrap up their summary with an idea that will make readers continue to think about the topic. In their wrap-up, students can use a question, a reference to an event, a quote, or a short anecdote.

   For "Deadly Drought" I could end in a question: What can you as a U.S. citizen do to increase our freshwater supply?

   For "New Frontiers" I could end in a reference to a historical event such as Wounded Knee.

FOLLOWING UP

- Continue to have students practice taking notes with the 5 W's Organizer.

- Have students write a summary with information you'd like them to recall, as writing supports understanding and remembering. Not every completed 5 W's Organizer should be turned into a summary.

LESSON 14

Collaborative Review Sheet

PURPOSE

To show students how working together is an excellent way to study, review, and create potential test questions

MATERIALS

Any completed chapter in a textbook or unit of study; Collaborative Review Sheet for a Unit or Chapter Test reproducible (page 89)

TIME

10 to 15 minutes during three consecutive classes

PRESENTING THE LESSON

TIME TO STUDY

1. Name the activity and explain how it helps students review and study for a test and create a plan that budgets their study time. Here's what I say:

   This activity invites you to work as a group and figure out what's important to study and learn for a test. Before taking notes, discuss with your group each prompt on the sheet. When completed, you will have detailed notes to study for your test, as well as possible questions that might appear on the test. Working as a group makes the review process richer and helps you remember important information.

2. Organize students into groups of four to six.

3. Give each group a review sheet from page 89 and separate notebook paper for them to write on.

4. Encourage students to look back in their textbooks and at any notes they've taken (or other materials) to ensure that their responses are accurate and specific.

5. Circulate around the room to observe groups and provide support when necessary.

6. Encourage students to help one another so that they collect detailed review notes.

7. Collect suggested test questions from students and make copies so that students have the questions their classmates wrote for studying.

FOLLOWING UP

- Have students review collaboratively before each unit test and before a final exam.

- To show that you value their thinking, use on your test some of the questions they generate.

TIME TO STUDY

This collaborative review starts the studying process for students and shows them what a review is like. Make sure that you give students one or two nights to study the material before the test. Doing this will help students experience success and the benefits of preparation and study.

Teach Students to Ask Open-Ended Questions

Explain that open-ended questions invite students to share their thinking about a topic, whereas factual questions call for memorized terms, dates, or names. Encourage students to create open-ended questions by teaching them the difference between the two types through example.

A factual question has only one answer.

Examples: *What kind of freshwater is in an unusable form? Who led the "Corps of Discovery"?*

An open-ended question has more than one answer.

Words such as *why, how, evaluate, infer,* and *compare/contrast* signal open-ended questions. Examples*: Why does fossil fuel pollution pose problems to freshwater supplies? How was this expedition treacherous and grueling?*

LESSON 15
Forming a Hypothesis and Supporting It

PURPOSE

To show students how to develop a hypothesis and support it with details from a text; to show students how their "hypothesis-support" notes can be a plan for writing an opinion paragraph

MATERIALS

"Drip Dry: Is It Possible That America's Water Sources Could One Day Be Tapped Out?" (pages 74–75); "Lewis & Clark: Journey Into the Unknown" (pages 76–78); or a short text on any topic to be studied in science or social studies; a class set of the Planner: Form a Hypothesis and Support It! reproducible (page 90); a class set of the Plan Your Opinion Paragraph reproducible (page 91)

TIME

15 minutes to develop and support a hypothesis

PRESENTING THE LESSON

1. Name the activity and explain how it helps students learn to develop a hypothesis and support it, then create a writing plan for an opinion paragraph. Here's what I say:

    This activity invites you to form a hypothesis based on the information you've read and studied. You'll learn how to state a hypothesis or opinion positively and negatively, then take notes to support each position. You'll reflect on your reading, skim and reread passages, and use details and inferences to try to support both the positive and negative positions. Doing this enables you to evaluate whether you have enough support to state that only one or both positions are valid based on your text(s). Then, you can choose the position you believe in and use your notes to plan and write a paragraph or short essay that describes it.

2. Explain to students that a hypothesis is an opinion, and that every opinion statement can be expressed in a positive and negative way. Let them know that it's a good mental exercise to learn to defend two opposite perspectives. Sometimes, students will find that they believe in the negative (or positive) stance, but can't find enough support for it. Looking at both sides of a hypothesis, then evaluating the support, will help students choose a position that's defendable.

3. Model how you use information in "Drip Dry" or in "Lewis & Clark" to form a hypothesis from a positive and negative point of view, then find support for each one.

64

Set a standard of needing three pieces of support for a hypothesis to be valid. Then evaluate the support. There's more than one hypothesis that can be developed from these and other selections, but I will share one.

For "Drip Dry," here's the hypotheses and support that I write on chart paper:

POSITIVE HYPOTHESIS	SUPPORT IT!
• *There will be enough water for people in our country in future years.*	• *If desalination becomes cheap, then there will be enough water. Right now it's very costly.* • *We can curb daily use by people through more efficient appliances and by not allowing watering of lawns.*
NEGATIVE HYPOTHESIS	**SUPPORT IT!**
• *There will not be enough water for people in our country in future years.*	• *Droughts diminish our water supply.* • *By 2080 the U.S. population will double and we'll need more water—water supplies are tight now.* • *Pollution of rivers, fossil fuel pollution, and global warming all reduce freshwater supplies*

Evaluation: The negative position is stronger because I have three convincing pieces of support. The positive statement really has only one piece of support because finding cheap ways to remove salt from the oceans is only a possibility. Therefore, the negative position is stronger, based on the information in "Drip Dry."

For "Lewis & Clark," here's the hypotheses and support that I write on chart paper:

POSITIVE HYPOTHESIS	SUPPORT IT!
• *The Native Americans that Lewis and Clark met helped make their journey a success.*	• *Sacagawea, a Shoshone Indian, helped the Corps cross the Rocky Mountains. She helped the Corps find roots and vegetables so they wouldn't starve.* • *When other tribes saw and spoke to Sacagawea, they understood that the Corps came in peace.* • *The Nez Perce fed the Corps near the end of their journey and helped the explorers build canoes for the last part of their journey.*
NEGATIVE HYPOTHESIS	**SUPPORT IT!**
• *The Native Americans that Lewis and Clark met did not help make their journey a success.*	• *There is no proof in this article for this statement.*

Evaluation: The only valid hypothesis is the positive one, for there are three convincing pieces of support for it and none for the negative one.

65

4. Give each student a copy of Planner: Form a Hypothesis and Support It! on page 90 and ask them to complete it after a unit of study.

ON ANOTHER DAY

Writing a Paragraph to Support a Hypothesis

1. Display the completed hypothesis–support chart you created for "Drip Dry" or "Lewis & Clark."
2. Show students how to turn their hypothesis into a topic sentence.
3. Give each student a copy of Plan Your Opinion Paragraph on page 91.
4. Ask students to use the Support It! details to complete their plan.
5. Before asking students to take notes for the closing, explain that an effective wrap-up should keep readers thinking about the defended position (see box above).

> Here are the notes that I write for "Drip Dry."
>
> *End with a question—What can you do to help enlarge our freshwater supply?*
>
> Here are the notes that I write for "Lewis and Clark."
>
> *End by asking readers to think about why the explorers named a stream after Sacagawea.*

6. Ask students to reread the paragraph and create a title for it.
7. Invite students to turn their Form a Hypothesis and Support It! notes into a writing plan, using the form on page 91.
8. Read students' plans before they write to make sure there are enough details.
9. Have students use their plans to write a paragraph.

Teach Students to Write a Wrap-up Sentence

A wrap-up is short, two to three sentences, and should leave readers with ideas to think about. Here are some questions and prompts that can help students find an idea to include in the wrap-up. Post them on chart paper so students have a resource to refresh their memories.

- Did you surprise the reader with an unusual fact or idea that relates to your piece?
- Does the wrap-up leave you thinking about the topic?
- Close with a thought-provoking question or a quote from an authority.
- Close with a short anecdote or story that relates to your topic.

Continue to Think About . . .

Asking your students to reflect on what they've read and experienced and then write about it benefits their recall, understanding, and ability to connect ideas and understand why the information is important. The activities in this chapter not only help students learn your content; they can also be used as assessments that can replace tests and/or be used in addition to tests. Before moving on to the last chapter, set aside time to reflect on the questions that follow. These questions will enable you to evaluate where you are with writing to think and learn after students have read their material.

- Why is it important to reserve time after reading for students to discuss material? How often do I do this?

- How many times do I demonstrate the note-taking and thinking processes for students? What do I do for students who find note taking a challenge?

- When do I have students collaborate, at school, to review for upcoming tests? How do I use their review sheets?

- Hoes do my demonstrations of writing to learn new material help my students learn content?

- Can I give examples of writing to learn new material in my classes?

- How often do I set aside time to help students understand the expectations for an activity before they complete it? Why is this important?

CHAPTER 5

Using Primary Sources to Motivate Readers

Connect Learners to Content and Enlarge Their Understanding

Primary resources such as letters, diary entries, cartoons, photographs, oral histories, excerpts from Supreme Court decisions, recordings of speeches, posters, legal papers, and official documents can help students relate to a historical period such as colonial America or a movement such as civil rights. Primary sources can also help learners gain insights into the lives of scientists and historical figures by reading their letters or diaries, and by seeing the connections between history and science when studying, for instance, the plague, yellow fever, or sanitation.

Dick Bell, a middle school history teacher at Powhatan School in Boyce, Virginia, uses primary sources with his seventh- and eighth-grade students. His responses to interview questions on page 70 show why Mr. Bell is strongly committed to integrating primary sources into his units of study.

The chapter discusses the benefits of using primary sources, especially in social studies, where more is available for middle school students. You'll find a form on page 92 that helps students read, evaluate, and think about a primary source, as well as examples of student responses.

The Difference Between Primary and Secondary Sources

The Response to Primary Sources sheet (page 92) can help students navigate primary documents.

Before introducing primary sources to your students, it's important to let them know the difference between primary and secondary sources. Explain that primary sources are documents created by people who were there and had firsthand knowledge of the event. Examples are letters, diaries, memoirs, autobiographies, posters, photographs, political cartoons, and newspaper articles. Often, primary sources—such as legal decrees, Supreme Court decisions, and speeches—are written later, when laws emerge from an event.

People who write informational books, history textbooks, biographies, newspaper articles, movies, and plays—people who did not experience and live through an event—are writing secondary sources. They write based on research of firsthand accounts and other secondary sources. It's important for students to understand that writers of secondary sources can manipulate or omit key information to present their take on an event, a person's life, or a historical period.

Integrating primary sources into your curriculum can give students a more accurate picture of an event or a person's life.

Primary Sources in Action: Seventh Grade

Since Dick Bell and his seventh graders were studying the Civil War, I adapted the Response to Primary Sources form (page 92) for that unit of study. Once students have gained some background knowledge of this period by using their textbook, Mr. Bell organizes students into pairs and introduces their study of primary sources. In addition to collecting from the Internet letters written by Confederate and Union soldiers and family members, Mr. Bell also uses materials from Primary Source Teaching Kit: *Civil War* by Karen Baicker (2003).

First, Mr. Bell discusses the difference between primary and secondary sources. Then, depending on the unit of study, Mr. Bell sets aside two or three class periods for students to pore over primary sources, using about 30 minutes of each 45-minute class period. Here's what the teaching and learning process looks like:

- Model, using the form students will use, how you respond to a primary source.

- Give partners a copy of the primary source and the response form.

- Allow students 15 to 20 minutes to share and write their responses.

- Pairs share during a whole-class discussion (about ten minutes).

- At the end of the week, students write, in their journals, what they have learned about the Civil War from their shared conversations about primary sources.

Interview With History Teacher, Dick Bell

Question: *Why do you use primary sources in history?*

Bell: Because it's the real deal: unsullied, uninterpreted by later historians. In the real voice of the times as it was, reflecting that age's prejudices, issues, and values.

Question: *What benefits do you see for your students?*

Bell: They get to meet the people of that time, to hear their voices (in the case of film, to see their aspects), to learn how their lives intersected with the issues and events of their times.

Question: *How do students respond to using primary sources?*

Bell: I remember using some soldiers' letters from the Civil War to try and humanize the faces of some of the combatants—no grand strategies, no smoke and shot-filled battlefields. There was this one Georgian named Moody. He was a sergeant, and he missed his wife and four kids terribly. He wrote these sad and highly illiterate letters home (the kids would have to decipher the spelling just to read them), and his wife would write the same kinds of letters back. In the last one he wrote, he told her that there was no reason he could understand for the war. He asked for her to send anything, anything that would be a reminder of their time together. He asked her to make him a pair of trousers for the marching season. She did. In the pockets of the trousers, she sewed a piece of her dress so she would always be right next to him. The trousers and her letter arrived after he had died in the Battle of Seven Pines. The students were deeply affected by this. That's the power of using primary sources.

Question: *How do primary sources improve students' understanding of history?*

Bell: Above all else, it gives them a personal context to connect to. Also, it hasn't been parsed and sieved for them. They mine for themselves the important material.

Question: *What additional advice do you have for teachers?*

Bell: It's great for forming hypotheses, then defending them in a debate or an opinion essay. Students appreciate historians, authors of primary sources, who make the right call. For example, my current seventh grade believes that the Sons of Liberty pushed the Revolutionary War principally because of economic reasons: Northern merchants who wanted their piece of that British mercantile pie and Southern plantation owners who wanted to skip out on huge personal indebtedness. Students take sides on this issue, which pushes them to do more research to defend their position. Sparks fly during debates or when students share their essays, creating an electrifying atmosphere for studying history.

I've included the pair-share reproducible that Mr. Bell's students used along with some sample responses by students. Note that the reading level is easy and accessible to all students, enabling learners to apply strategies independently and focus on content.

Students' responses reveal developing empathy for Civil War soldiers and for the hospitals that treated the wounded. This deepened understanding would not have occurred if the textbook were students' only source. According to Loewen (1995) and Zarnowski (2006), history textbooks try to cover far too many topics and stick to the facts, leaving out personal stories and controversial material. When textbooks fail to help students experience a period or event, primary sources (and poetry) can close that gap.

Sorrel's responses to the letter written by Private John F. Brobst (see Figure 5.1 on page 72) shows the level of thinking and the connections she made to her experiences based on this letter (see page 93 for the letter). When Sorrel writes, "I can understand how he feels. The letter connects me because of the missing home point. Every year I go to camp, and miss home, and get reminded of it [the missing part] often."

In Figure 5.2 on page 72, Mei responds to a selection from "Diary of a Georgia Girl, 1864" (see page 94) and points repeatedly to the position of women during this historical period—not a threat to either side. Mei points out that she learned how strongly people felt about the war and that soldiers don't think about the fact that they leave dead animals behind.

Name _____ Date _____

Pair/Share/Write/Learn
from Your Civil War Document!

TITLE OR NAME AND AUTHOR OF THE DOCUMENT:

DATE OF THE DOCUMENT:

IDENTIFY THE KIND OF DOCUMENT YOU HAVE:

Discuss the document with your partner using these questions:

1. What do you think is the purpose of this document? What did the author want you to think, understand, and feel?

2. What side or group does the document defend or support? What information or words in the document make you think this?

3. What information about slavery, soldiers, politics, economics, or people's attitudes do you learn from your document?

4. How does this document connect you to the period in history? What in the document helped you make these connections?

5. What conclusions can you draw about how the North or the South might react to this document?

6. How does the document make you feel about the Civil War and war in general? Explain.

Now that you've discussed the document with your partner, write your responses on the back of this sheet or on a piece of separate notebook paper.

Pair-Share Response Form used in Civil Way unit. Sample student responses to letters and diaries written during the war appear on page 72.

Thomas, responding to "Diary of a Georgia Girl" (see Figure 5.3 on page 72), astutely concludes that "The North might look back on this [the diary] and be upset with themselves, the South would just have their memories refreshed and become more enraged." Thomas's wish that "we could have just made it [the Civil War] a 'verbal war'" mirrors the reactions of many students who thought of the heroism associated with war, but not of the toll on human life.

Kaleigh's responses in Figure 5.4 (page 72) to "Hospitals and the Wounded: Clara Barton" (see page 95) show her understanding of and empathy for the wounded who needed medical care. She points out that images such as "wet, bloody floors" enabled her to see the problem of not having enough hospitals or people to care for soldiers and the fact that the South didn't want to care for the wounded Union soldiers.

71

① The purpose of this letter is to express the difficulties of being a soldier. I think that because he says so much about the extra weight that he has to carry and how he misses home.

② The letter was written by a union soldier, but I dont think that you would be able to tell the diffrence b/c they both go through the same things.

③ I learned that although there are many supporters to the wars and both the sides that are competing, there still isnt much money to use in terms of food and clothing. He said he ate about half a meal for every two days.

④ I can understand how he feels. The letter connects me because of the missing home part. Every year I go to camp, and miss home, and get reminded of it often

⑤ The North would be saddened about this letter. It shows to them how hard a soldiers life is because they cant find alot of money to treat them They would also be Proud. Their soldiers are suffering, but they are still holding on to their patriotism. The South would be hopeful that their soldiers are doing the same.

⑥ The war seems like a terrible thing to do, but I know is has to be done. I know there are people who want to have it, so they can prove to their country how tough they are. So they can feel the pain of patriotism.

Figure 5.1 *Sorrel's responses to the letter written by Private John F. Brobst*

1) I think the purpose of this document is to remind herself of what she saw and felt that day after she saw some of the remains of Sherman's March. But, because this is a diary entry I don't think she expected it to be seen.

2) This document supports the South, we can tell because it says she's from Georgia and she wants to hang a Yankee (soldier).

3) I learned that people felt very strongly about their views on the war. It also shows that soldiers don't think about the way they leave things, they destroyed everything the south had, their agriculture.

4) This connects me to that period in history because she is recalling what she's seen and it feels like you're with her.

5) The North wouldn't think about her very much, she's only a female, and they would be proud some of their boys left the South in such ruin, the south however would agree that what the North did was horrible and they ought to be punished, but where was their army? Why wasn't their army protecting them?

6) This makes me feel like war is terrible and hard. Why couldn't things be settled peacefully. And not only is war hard for the soldiers, war is hard on everyone.

Figure 5.2 *Mei's responses to a selection from "Diary of a Georgia Girl, 1864"*

① The purpose of this document is to display the ruindness of the town's that had been ivaded + destroyed.

② The document defends the South Mainly because of what the North had done, left the town bare and ruined so much so that even a northerner would find it apualling.

③ I learned People's attitudes towards the actions of the North, like Eliza's opinion, that it would be a terrible act and the People that did it were "infamous wretches".

④ By describing the ruins and it measuring objects we don't use today.

The North might look back on this and be
⑥ upset w/ themselves, the South would just have their memorys refreshed and become more enraged.

⑦ again these documents make war seem so terrible + crulE I wish we could have just made it a verbal war?

Figure 5.3 *Thomas's responses to "Diary of a Georgia Girl, 1864"*

1. I think the purpose of this document was to inform people of what life was like to be a wounded solider in the Civil war, how bad it was, and how miserable life was. "Begging me in Heaven's name for a cracker..."

2. I support the union because, at the bottom, it states that the "houses were opened to the 'dirty, lousy, soliders' of the Union Army"

3. It has information about soliders and I learned that it was horrible life to be a wounded solider in the Civil war, and most people would rather die than go through the pain.

4. It connects me to the period in history by using very specific details about the war. Like "Wet, bloody floors" or "a cup they might have something to drink water from.

5. They might be sad because all of their soliders are getting wounded. The south would be happy that they were winning and killing and wounding the north.

6. that it was a very sad place and not many people made it out of there without a wound (or being dead).

Figure 5.4 *Kaleigh's responses to "Hospitals and the Wounded: Clara Barton"*

Bring Poetry to Science and Social Studies

Pat Lewis has created poems that relate to what you teach in history, geography, and science in a topnotch book called *Poems for Teaching in the Content Areas: 75 Powerful Poems to Enhance Your History, Geography, Science, and Math Lessons*. You can simply use the poems in read-alouds to build background knowledge and motivate students to learn more about a topic. Or you can have groups collaborate to understand a poem's meaning and implications, then teach it to their classmates.

Introducing each section in this book is a list of easy-to-implement teaching ideas that I created for you to use or adapt to your students' needs.

The facts listed in a textbook could not develop the connections, emotional ties, and understanding that these primary sources did, enabling young adults to enter an important period in our history and deepen their understanding of it. What's exciting is to observe students change their attitudes toward war based on the viewpoints that primary sources present.

Continue to Think About . . .

As you focus on helping students learn the content in your social studies or science curriculum, set aside ten minutes three times a week to model and teach strategies that can improve students' reading, understanding, and recall. Once you're comfortable with introducing reading and vocabulary-building strategies, consider weaving primary sources and poetry into your studies.

RESOURCES FOR PRIMARY SOURCES

Primary Sources Kits by Karen Baicker, published by Scholastic

- *Civil Rights* (2003)
- *Civil War* (2003)
- *Colonial America* (2002)
- *Explorers* (2002)
- *Immigration* (2003)
- *The Westward Movement* (2002)

Primary sources published by Heinemann

- *In Pursuit of Freedom: Teaching the Underground Railroad* by William Kashatus (2005)
- *Making Freedom: African Americans in U.S. History,* Primary Source Inc. (2004)
- *Our New Day Begun: 1861–1877 (Sourcebook 4)* Primary Source Inc. (2004)

73

Drip, Dry?

Is it possible that America's water could one day be tapped out?

BY SEAN PRICE

Across much of the United States, the days of carefree water use are long gone. Take for instance Denver's Water World: The theme park sells cold soft drinks, but those who want ice in theirs have to ask for it. Why the hassle? Park officials discovered that giving ice only on request saves about 30,000 gallons of water each year—enough to fill two backyard swimming pools.

Such water-stingy behavior seems unusual to most Americans, who are used to cheap, plentiful H2O. But more and more people are finding that the 341 billion gallons that the nation uses daily can no longer be taken for granted. Overuse, *drought* (below-normal rainfall and snowfall), water-wasting technology, and pollution are sapping the supply. Meanwhile, demand for water continues to surge.

WATER WORLD

How could a liquid that covers to thirds of Earth be in short supply? There are two main reasons, says Peter Gleick, a water expert at the research group Pacific Institute: First, 97 percent of the world's water is saltwater—useless for drinking or nurturing crops unless expensive desalination techniques are used to purify it. Second, much of the remaining freshwater is either in an unusable form, like glaciers, or unevenly distributed due to geography and climate (average weather in an area over time).

"The fact that there's a lot of water in the Great Lakes doesn't help people in Arizona." Gleick. says.

Today, rivers, lakes, and underground *aquifers* (rocks that contain water) are equipped to supply freshwater to the country's 295 million people. But the population is expected to double by about the 2080s. "As populations grow, you're going to run into a limit to your resources," says Steve Vandas, a hydrologist with the U. S. Geological Survey.

SUSTAINING SUPPLIES

To keep up with demand, U.S. waterways must stay clean. Just decades ago, waterways were so polluted with chemicals that one actually caught on fire. Thanks to tough antipollution laws like the Clean Water Act of 1972, many factories stopped treating rivers and lakes like garbage dumps. Robbi Savage, president of World Water Monitoring Day, says some of the most pervasive pollution now comes from household chemicals such as oil and pesticides.

Reducing household pollutants can help. But we also need to use less water, says Gleick. "We can grow food, get rid of waste, and [run factories] with less water—without harming our quality of life," he says. "We're not always using the smartest tools to do the job. We still waste tremendous amounts of water." *Read on to learn what's tapping your freshwater supply.*

 © 2009 Laura Robb Scholastic Professional

DOWN AND OUT

In 1999, the western states entered their worst drought in 500 years. Water reservoirs along the Colorado River have since dropped to half their normal levels. That's critical for the 25 million people in seven states who rely on the river's water. However, the drought has inspired millions of people to switch to using water-saving toilets and washing machines. The efforts have worked so well in Denver that water consumption rates currently are at their lowest levels in 30 years.

HOW IS WATER USED IN THE UNITED STATES?

A. What percentage of water is used for drinking and home use?

B. What steps could you take to stem the flow in your house?

HIGH AND DRY

Explosive Population growth around Atlanta, Georgia, is outstripping the water supply in the Southeast. This has triggered a legal fight among three states. Georgia wants to pump more water from the Chattahoochee River. Two downstream states—Alabama and Florida—argue that the extra water removal will leave them high and dry.

WATER HAZARD

Burning *fossil fuels*, such as coal and oil, emits air pollutants. U.S. autos produce 8.2 million tons of nitrogen oxide a year. This, along with sulfur dioxide and other pollutants, makes *acid rain*. *Precipitation*—rain, snow, hail, or sleet—mixes with the poisons and slowly kills plants and fish.

WEB EXTRA

For more on water basics and acid rain, visit http://ga.water.usgs.gov/edu/

POTENT POLLUTION

Water pollution threats come from many sources including animal manure and chemicals. For instance, underground gasoline tanks have been leaking *methyl tertiary butyl ether* (MTBE) into groundwater in 49 states. MTBE makes gasoline burn cleaner, but it can cause cancer when consumed. Additionally, chemicals like nitrogen and phosphorous found in fertilizers and factory pollution regularly wash into the Mississippi River. The pollutants deprive fish of oxygen. The result: a 7,000-square-mile "dead zone" around the river's mouth.

WARM WARNINGS

Scientists believe that air pollution magnifies Earth's natural greenhouse effect, causing global warming (average increase in Earth's temperature). In California's Sierra Nevada, winter precipitation that once came down as snow now falls as rain. The snow used to melt gradually, delivering water to thirsty Californians during near-rainless summers. Now, the water runs into waterways at once, leaving less for the dry months. This year, rain fell in bucketfuls, washing out to sea.

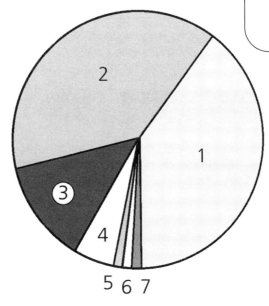

1. Irrigation: 40%
2. Thermoelectric power: 39%
3. Drinking and home use: 13%
4. Industry: 5%
5. Livestock: 1%
6. Commercial: 1%
7. Mining: 1%

Source: U.S. Geological Survey

LEWIS & CLARK

❋ Journey Into the Unknown ❋

A group of daring explorers headed west from Missouri nearly 200 years ago. Their journey would change the U.S. forever.

by Matt Warshauer

"We shall delineate [mark] with correctness the great arteries [rivers] of this great country," wrote President Thomas Jefferson in 1805. "Those who come after will fill up the canvas we begin."

Jefferson had long cultivated a fascination with the West. His library contained more volumes on the region than any library in the world. Jefferson also foresaw a United States that would stretch from sea to sea. To achieve this goal, the U.S., he knew, would have to establish a solid claim to its western territories.

As President, Jefferson got the chance to realize his dreams of westward expansion. In January 1803, he obtained $2,500 from the U.S. Congress to fund a journey to the Pacific Coast. Three months later, the U.S. purchased the Louisiana Territory from France. An area of 827,987 square miles stretching from the Mississippi River to the Rocky Mountains, it doubled the size of the nation.

Sacagawea interprets Lewis and Clark's intentions to the Chinook Indians.

President Jefferson chose Meriwether Lewis, his personal secretary, to lead a "Corps of Discovery" across thousands of miles of territory. Lewis, in turn, asked William Clark, under whom he had served in the Frontier Army, to be his co-captain.

Clark happily accepted the challenge. "My friend," he wrote, "I join you with hand & Heart."

Starting Out

A warm spring rain fell on May 14, 1804, when the Corps of Discovery set off from the banks of the tiny Wood River, near St. Louis, Missouri (see map). About 50 men crossed the Mississippi River in a keelboat (large flat-bottomed boat) and two pirogues (canoe-like boats). Sixteen of the men would return home before the expedition reached the Pacific Ocean. Only one, Sergeant Charles Floyd, would die along the way, probably of a ruptured appendix.

The Corps headed up the Missouri River, battling its strong currents. On land, the expedition encountered animals

Voyage of Discovery Time Line

William Clark

>>MAY 14, 1804 Members of the Corps of Discovery head West from Missouri "under a jentle brease," as Clark writes.

>>SEPTEMBER 25, 1804 Teton Sioux Indians demand one of the explorers' boats in exchange for permission to travel farther up the Missouri River. A fight is narrowly avoided.

>>NOVEMBER 4, 1804 Lewis and Clark hire a French Canadian trader, Toussaint

Charbonneau, as an interpreter. His Shoshone wife, Sacagawea, also joins the expedition.

>>APRIL 29, 1805 Lewis and one of the other men kill an enormous grizzly bear.

>>JUNE 13, 1805 Lewis encounters "the grandest sight I ever beheld"—the Great Falls of the Missouri.

>>AUGUST 17, 1805 The explorers buy horses from a band of Shoshone Indians.

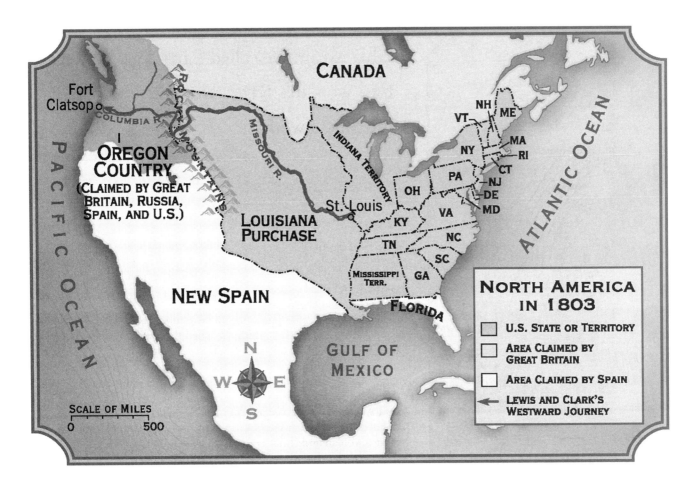

NORTH AMERICA IN 1803

- ☐ U.S. STATE OR TERRITORY
- ☐ AREA CLAIMED BY GREAT BRITAIN
- ☐ AREA CLAIMED BY SPAIN
- ← LEWIS AND CLARK'S WESTWARD JOURNEY

none of the men had ever seen, including grizzly bears, bighorn sheep, and buffalo. The Corps endured scorching heat, heavy rains, frigid temperatures, and relentless mosquitoes. Throughout their journey, the men were, by turns, sick, exhausted, and half-starved.

Words to Know

Continental Divide: a series of mountain ridges extending from Alaska to Mexico that form the watershed of North America

Says historian Dayton Duncan: "The group came face-to-face with gigantic disappointments, but they continued on- one day at a time, one paddle stroke after another."

In what is now North Dakota, the captains hired a French Canadian trader, Toussaint Charbonneau, to serve as an interpreter with Indian tribes. Charbonneau brought his young Shoshone Indian wife, Sacagawea (sah-KAG-ah-way-ah), then six months pregnant. Lewis and Clark thought Sacagawea could help them buy horses from Shoshones who lived at the headwaters (source of a river) of the

Missouri. But her importance to the journey would far surpass that.

Chronicling the West

The voyage provided countless remarkable sights for the Corps. Lewis wrote of the White Cliffs in presentday Montana: "As we passed on, it seemed as if those scenes of enchantment would never have an end."

Lewis recorded this observation along with many others in journals he and the crew kept. Of all the items the explorers brought back, these first-person accounts of the voyage and its wonders may have been the most valuable.

Their chief turns out to be Sacagawea's brother, Cameahwait, whom she had not seen since childhood.

>>SEPTEMBER 22, 1805 Members of the Corps emerge from the Bitterroot Mountains.

>>NOVEMBER 7, 1805 Clark writes that "we are in *view* of the *Ocian*." It is actually 20 miles away.

>>MARCH 23, 1806 After a rainy winter

near present-day Astoria, Oregon, the group heads home—for a time taking two separate routes.

>>JULY 27, 1806 Lewis's group kills two Blackfeet Indians in a skirmish over horses, the only violent deaths during the expedition.

>>SEPTEMBER 23, 1806 The explorers arrive back in St. Louis to the cheers of townspeople.

Meriwether Lewis

> "this stream we called Sâh-câ-ger we-âh or bird woman's River, after our interpreter the Snake woman."
>
> Meriwether Lewis

"Great Father"

Clark was the group's chief cartographer (mapmaker). He filled his journals with detailed maps of the lands, mountains, and rivers through which the Corps traveled. Lewis was the team's scientific expert. He identified some 178 plants and 122 animals that were new to scientists, including the coyote and the porcupine.

Lewis and Clark also made important studies of almost 50 Indian tribes living in the western U.S. Jefferson had instructed Lewis to establish "friendly" contact with the tribes. The explorers told the Indians that President Jefferson was their new "Great Father," and that the Indian nations were part of the U.S.

Lewis and Clark depended on many Indian tribes for guidance and survival. But no one was more important to their success than Sacagawea.

She helped the Corps endure the treacherous (dangerous) crossing of the Rocky Mountains, and taught them how to dig for edible (fit to be eaten) roots and vegetables. When a sudden storm tipped over a canoe, she calmly plucked supplies, including the group's journals, from the rapids.

Sacagawea, which means "Bird Woman," also served as a symbol of peace. Other Indians, seeing a woman and child, understood that the white men were not a war party.

"Immense Ranges"

In the late summer of 1805, the expedition had been through one its most difficult periods. Circling the Great Falls of Montana and climbing the Rocky Mountains had taken three grueling (exhausting) months.

On August 12, 1805, Lewis's scouting party reached the Continental Divide-the crest of the Rockies-near present-day Lemhi, Idaho. On the other side, Lewis expected to see a vast valley and the Columbia River leading away to the Pacific Ocean. Instead, all he saw were more "immense ranges of high mountains."

It was a great disappointment. There was no easy water route to the Pacific-only more hard traveling. After 11 long days of struggle through the Bitterroot Mountains, the Corps finally emerged at the site of present-day Weippe, Idaho. Again, friendly Indians saved them. The Nez Perce (nehz PURS) fed the Corps-who had survived on a few grouse, a raven, and a coyote, among other animals-and helped them build canoes for the final leg of their trip.

"America's Future"

In November 1805, the Corps finally reached the Pacific Coast. They built Fort Clatsop (in present-day Oregon), where they spent a rainy and miserable winter.

Although the journey to the Pacific took more than a year and a half, the trip home would only take six months. Many people back East thought the expedition members were dead. So it was with great excitement-and shock-that St. Louis residents welcomed the Corps of Discovery back on September 23, 1806.

"The people gathred on the Shore and [gave us] three cheers," wrote Sergeant John Ordway of the return.

Filmmaker Ken Burns calls Lewis and Clark's epic journey "the most important expedition in the history of the U.S." The explorers, he adds, "saw America's future. They charted where we would go."

Your Turn

WORD MATCH

1. treacherous   A. source of a river
2. edible   B. dangerous
3. grueling   C. fit to be eaten
4. headwaters   D. mapmaker
5. cartographer   E. exhausting

THINK ABOUT IT

In what ways was Lewis and Clark's journey a success? In what ways did it spell doom for many Indian tribes?

© 2009 Laura Robb   Scholastic Professional

Essential Questions for Science and Social Studies

Here is a list of questions that link students to issues in science and social studies. My hope is that these questions will serve as models so that you and your students can create essential queries that drive students' learning.

SCIENCE

- Is our water supply dwindling? If so, how can we prevent supplies from shrinking?

- Is global warming a threat to humans and all of the natural world? If so, how can we prevent it or reduce its effects? If not, why does this problem receive so much media attention?

- How do natural resources influence human society?

- How can we conserve our limited energy supplies?

- Is space a viable frontier?

- Why does humankind need to understand Earth?

- Why is going green important to Earth and mankind? What are the consequences of not going green?

- What role do you students play in your ecological future?

- Is nuclear energy a safe option?

- Is it important to maintain biodiversity on Earth? Why or why not?

- Explain how and why a union of countries throughout the world can save the future of this earth?

- Is cloning contaminating our food supply? Explain your position.

- How can we diminish fossil fuel emissions?

- Are pandemics preventable? Explain your position.

- Are cars a necessity in our world? Take a position and explain it.

- Why are trees, forests, parks, and open land important to the planet and all who inhabit it?

SOCIAL STUDIES

- What drives humans to want more money, land, and power?

- Why do we study ancient civilizations today?

- What does a "good citizen" look like? How can we develop such citizens?

- Why is it important to understand different cultures from the past and in the present?

- Is a democratic republic the best form of government for the United States? Defend your position if your response is "yes." Otherwise, suggest an alternate form of government and explain why that is your preference.

- Is government necessary? Use your knowledge of past and present governments from different countries and current events to frame your defense.

- What role does economics play in our government's decisions? Give examples.

- Is war inevitable? Explain how humans can learn to resolve differences in peaceful ways.

- What challenges do people face who live in large urban areas of our country today? How can these problems be solved?

- How can we conquer the racial divide that still exists in America?

- Why are laws important in a democracy? Can there be just laws in a totalitarian government?

List/Group/Label

Directions:

1. Discuss with your partner the topic of the new unit of study; write it on a separate sheet of paper.

2. Brainstorm a list of words and phrases you associate with the topic; record them on the paper.

3. Work with your partner and think of headings or categories that you could organize the words and phrases under.

4. Defend your decision to place some words under more than one heading.

Name _____ Date _____

Title and Pages _____

Rate Your Word Knowledge Chart

WORD	A SYNONYM I KNOW	I CAN DEFINE IT	SOME DETAILS I KNOW	THIS WORD IS UNFAMILIAR TO ME

Journal Page

Directions:

1. Set up a double-entry journal page on a separate sheet of paper. At the top of the page, write your name, date, title, and the pages you are reading. Then divide the paper into two columns.

2. Label the left-hand side "Questions" and write your questions underneath, leaving five or six lines after each one.

3. Label the right-hand column "Notes" and make notes that answer your questions as you read.

Concept Map

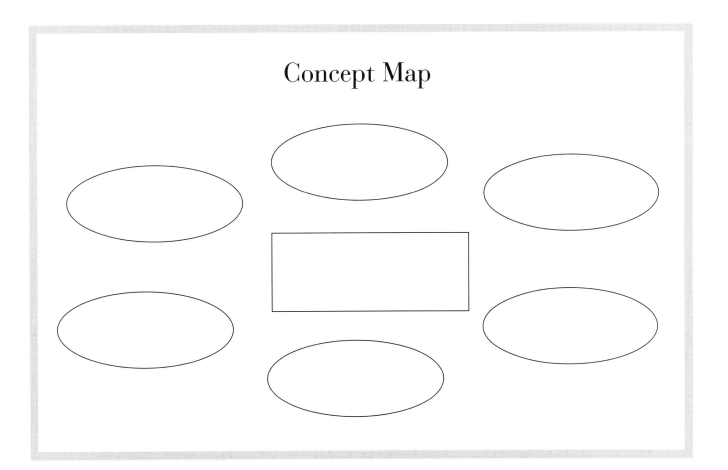

Name _____ Date _____

Title, Topic, and Pages _____

Word Analysis Map

WRITE THE WORD:	DEFINITION FROM CONTEXT:

PART OF SPEECH:

LIST SITUATIONS IN WHICH YOU WOULD USE THE WORD:

WHAT IS IT LIKE? LIST ANY FEATURES:

GIVE SOME RELATED EXAMPLES:

WRITE THE DICTIONARY DEFINITION THAT EXPLAINS THE WORD USED IN THE TEXT:

CHOOSE ONE OF THE SITUATIONS AND USE THE WORD IN A SENTENCE:

 © 2009 Laura Robb   Scholastic Professional

Guidelines to Help You
Close Read Tough Passages

CLOSE READ is a fix-up strategy that asks you to return to a confusing sentence or passage and reread it slowly and carefully. Focus on the following elements, and use the related questions to help you figure out their meaning.

ELEMENTS TO FOCUS ON	QUESTIONS TO FIGURE OUT THEIR MEANING
unfamiliar words	• Can I find clues in the passage or in diagrams, photos, and captions to figure out the word?
pronouns with unclear references	• Does the pronoun refer to a fact or name in the sentence? • Does the pronoun refer to a fact or name in an earlier sentence?
facts that don't seem connected	• Can I connect the facts in one sentence to the next sentence or the previous one? Do I have any knowledge I can connect to the facts?
long and complex sentences	• Can I use commas to break up a sentence and bring what I know to the details?
information that is unfamiliar	• Can I ask a peer to help me get the background knowledge I need?

Context Clues That Help You
Determine the Meaning of a Tough Word

Here are examples of context clues authors embed so readers can determine the meaning of tough words.

A CLEAR DEFINITION—The word's meaning follows a comma, dash, the word *or*, or the phrase *is called* or *are called*, or is in parentheses that come right after the word. *Example: Lewis and Clark thought Sacagawea could help them buy horses from Shoshones who lived at the headwaters (source of a river) of the Missouri.* (From "Lewis & Clark" by Matt Warshauer. In *Junior Scholastic,* Vol. 106, No. 7.)

A CONCRETE EXAMPLE—The example the author provides helps readers figure out the word's meaning. Connect *household chemicals* to *pervasive* and figure out what it means. *Example: Robbi Savage, president of World Water Monitoring Day, says some of the most* **pervasive** *pollution now comes from* **household chemicals** *such as oil and pesticides.* (From "Drip Dry" by Sean Price. In *Science World,* Vol. 61, No. 13.)

REPETITION OF A NEW WORD—Authors repeat a difficult word or concept in familiar and different situations. This helps readers get the meaning by using what they already know. *Example: America is a nation of* **immigrants**. **Immigrants** *are people who come to a new land to make their home. All Americans are related to* **immigrants** *or are* **immigrants** *themselves.* (From *Coming to America: The Story of Immigration*, unpaged picture book.)

IN OTHER SENTENCES—The clue is in sentences that come before and/or after the word. *Example: This, along with sulfur dioxide and other pollutants, makes* **acid rain**. *Precipitation—rain, snow, hail, or sleet—mixes with the poisons and slowly kills plants and fish.* (From "'Drip Dry" by Sean Price. In *Science World,* Vol. 61, No. 13.)

RESTATED MEANINGS—The author explains a tough word by restating its meaning. Commas can set off the restated meaning. You'll also find restatement after *or, that is,* or *in other words.* Sometimes the meaning is stated in sentences that follow, using examples that help you understand the meaning. *Example: The Corps* **endured** *scorching heat, heavy rains, frigid temperatures, and relentless mosquitoes. Throughout their journey, the men were by turns,* **sick, exhausted, and half-starved**. (From "Lewis & Clark" by Matt Warshauer. In *Junior Scholastic,* Vol. 106, No. 7.)

IN A NONFICTION FEATURE—Definitions of terms can be in captions, sidebars, diagrams, and so on. *Example: Scientists believe that air pollution magnifies Earth's natural greenhouse effect, causing* **global warming** *(average increase in Earth's temperature).* (In a sidebar from "Drip Dry" by Sean Price. In *Junior Scholastic,* Vol. 106, No. 7.)

Name _____ Date _____

Word Map

Directions:

1. *Under "What is it?" write the word or concept to review.*

2. *Come up with a similar word or phrase and write it in the box at the left.*

3. *Under "What is it like?" write four to six of its characteristics. Then write some examples in the space below.*

4. *After you complete the map, use the word in a sentence that shows you understand its meaning.*

WHAT IS IT?   WHAT IS IT LIKE?

1. _____

2. _____

3. _____

4. _____

5. _____

6. _____

EXAMPLES:

MY SENTENCE:

Tips for Taking Notes

Whenever your teacher asks you to take notes, review these guidelines. They will help you be more successful and will guide you to use your notes to analyze the information and make connections.

1. With your teacher, a classmate, or on your own, set purposes for reading. Having clear purposes helps you pinpoint important details that you can jot down, in your own words, as notes.

2. Take notes after you have read and understood the material. This allows you to write your notes in your own words and demonstrates your comprehension.

3. Reread your notes and discuss them with a partner or silently with yourself. Add extra details that you feel are important. You might have to skim some parts or reread passages at this stage.

4. Think about your notes and try to react to them by stating how the information makes you feel or by connecting the notes to other texts and experiences. You can use these prompts and questions to help you react and make connections:

    - *What does this information mean to me?*

    - *What feelings and thoughts does this information stir?*

    - *How does this information change the way I think?*

    - *Do I have more questions? What are they?*

5. Discuss your connections with a partner, small group, or the entire class.

6. Reread and study your notes so you remember the information.

   © 2009 Laura Robb   Scholastic Professional

Name _____ Date _____

Chapter Title and Pages _____

Question/Answer/Connect/React

Directions:

1. *Pose questions on the left-hand side of the paper before you read. Questions can be about new vocabulary, a photograph, a caption, a sidebar, a chart, a graph, or a diagram.*

2. *After reading, skim the text to find answers to your questions. Write your answers in the middle column in your own words.*

3. *Then write your connections and reactions on the right-hand side.*

QUESTIONS	ANSWERS	CONNECTIONS/REACTIONS

TIPS FOR MAKING
CONNECTIONS

Make connections to other topics, a movie, a video, a book, or a magazine article. Also think about why this information is important and how it can change lives.

Name _____ Date _____

5 W's Organizer

Directions:

1. Read the explanation of each of the five W's.

2. Take detailed notes in your own words under each heading.

WHO OR WHAT: *Who (or what) is this about?*

WHAT: *What happened?*

WHEN: *When did it happen?*

WHERE: *Where did it happen?*

WHY: *Why did it happen? Why is it significant? (Consider connections to self, other texts, technology, and community and world issues.)*

Chapter Title _____ Pages _____

Collaborative Review Sheet for a Unit or Chapter Test

Directions:

1. *Bring your notes and textbook to each group meeting.*

2. *Work together on each prompt on this sheet and help one another so that your answers are detailed and specific. Return to pages in the chapter and skim to refresh your memory.*

3. *Write your notes on separate paper or in your journal.*

4. *Turn in to your teacher any questions that your group feels need extra teaching and review.*

- List key vocabulary that you need to remember. Explain the meaning of each word and relate it to the topic. Do this in your own words.

- Draw and label diagrams and/or maps you need to remember.

- List all the key points that your teacher made in class that you believe may be on the test.

- List some items that you feel you'll be asked to identify and discuss. Complete each identification.

- Write all the inferences and connections you made based on your notes and a discussion with group members.

- List some factual questions you believe may be on the test.

- List some open-ended questions that you believe might be on the test. These can start with words such as *evaluate, why, how, explain, compare/contrast.*

- Make a plan below that shows how you will budget your study time:

> *Here are some suggestions you can follow or adapt:*
>
> - *I have ____nights to study prior to the test.*
>
> - *I will study my class notes and this review sheet for _____minutes each night.*
>
> - *I will practice drawing and labeling maps or diagrams that might be on the test.*
>
> - *I will think of answers to the test questions that all groups wrote.*

Name _____ Date _____

Planner: Form a Hypothesis and Support It!

Directions:

1. *Write the name of the text (a completed chapter, biography, or informational trade book) you will use to support your hypothesis below.*

2. *Form a hypothesis about the topic or person.*

3. *State your hypothesis from a positive and a negative point of view.*

4. *Search the text for three supporting details for each position. You'll need three pieces of support for a position to be valid.*

5. *Complete the question about validity, at the bottom of the page.*

Text: _____

POSITIVE HYPOTHESIS   SUPPORT IT!

NEGATIVE HYPOTHESIS   SUPPORT IT!

WHICH STATEMENTS ARE VALID? EXPLAIN YOUR ANSWER.

Name _____ Date _____

Plan Your Opinion Paragraph

Directions:

1. *Choose a hypothesis or opinion statement that you've created and supported with at least three details from the text.*

2. *Use the information that you collected and your reading materials to complete this form.*

POSSIBLE TITLE: *Come up with something that gives readers a clue to what you'll discuss; this can be changed or adjusted.*

TOPIC SENTENCE: *Use your hypothesis (opinion statement) to develop an interesting topic sentence.*

NOTES FOR THE BODY: *Elaborate and develop the three supporting details here. Be specific.*

NOTES FOR THE WRAP-UP OR CLOSING: *Try to add a new idea that grows out of your opinion.*

Once your teacher approves your plan, draft your paragraph or short essay on separate paper.

Name_____ _____Date_____

Response to Primary Sources

Title or Name and Author _____

Type of Document _____

Directions:

1. *Complete the silent reading of the document.*

2. *Think about your reading, then discuss it with a partner.*

3. *After your discussion, write your responses to each question that applies to your document. Use separate paper.*

DISCUSSION QUESTIONS:

1. What do you think is the purpose of the document? What did the author want you to think, understand, or feel?

2. What does this document mean to you?

3. What information did you learn? Be specific.

4. Does the writer have a concern? If so, what is that concern?

5. Can you identify the writer's tone? (Use verbs, repeated words and phrases, and specific images.)

6. How might other people who lived through this event or period have reacted to this document? Explain why.

7. How might people living today react to it? Explain why.

8. What connections did this document help you make? Be specific.

LETTERS HOME ABOUT SOLDIER LIFE
1864

Private John F. Brobst
[Union Soldier]
25th Wisconsin Infantry
Spring 1864

It is very hard to be a soldier. No matter how bad the weather is you must go. If it rains you must stand or sleep out, with not as much as a leaf to shelter you from the storm. Perhaps have about half a meal for two days, and that the poorest kind of living . . . . This is not the case at all times, for when we are where we can get it we have plenty, and that which is good. But most of the time we are on the move and then we cannot get such as is fit for a man to eat.

Now, I will tell you as near as I can what the load is that a soldier has to carry, and march from 15 to 25 miles a day. He as a gun that weighs 11 pounds, cartridges and cartridge box about 6 pounds, woolen blanket 3 pounds, canteen full of water which they oblige you to keep full all the time, which is about 6 pounds, then three or five days' rations, which will weigh about 8 pounds, and then your little trinkets that we need, perhaps 2 pounds, makes a total of about 45 or 50 pounds. That is what makes us think of our homes in these hot days.

Union soldier, 1861

Lieutenant John W. Comer
[Confederate Soldier]
45th Alabama Infantry
June 14, 1864

"I am glad to say that I am still safe & well. I never enjoyed better health in my life, I have a few sores on one of my feet, caused I think from such hard and continual marching. We have been on the [march] since . . . the 5th day of May. When we lie down at night we do not know how long we will be permitted to sleep, all the principle maneuvers are made in the night. I never think of pulling off my clothes or shoes when I lie down. I have not pulled off my pants or shoes to lie down more than twice since the 5th of May. I sleep with my belt around me & my sword & haversack under my head so as to be ready to move in a moment when called upon. . . .
I do not believe there is a soldier in this army but what has got lice (body lice I mean). I have got my clothes boiled [to get rid of the lice] but to no purpose. . . . They plague me half to death, keeping me scratching & feeling . . . While I am writing our pickets [advanced sentries] are fighting in front & the enemy are cannonading heavily. But I have become accustomed to the sound and it does not bother me at all. . . .

Lt. [John] Wallace Comer,
and Burrell, his 'body servant'

from Primary Sources Teaching Kit: *Civil War by Karen Baicker* (Scholastic, 2003)

"DIARY OF A GEORGIA GIRL"
1864

"December 24, 1864. —About three miles from Sparta [Georgia] *we struck the 'burnt country,' as it was well named by the natives, and then I could better understand the wrath and desperation of these poor people. I almost felt as if I should like to hang a Yankee myself. There was hardly a fence left standing all the way from Sparta to Gordon. The fields were trampled down and the road lined with carcasses of horses, hogs, and cattle that the invaders, unable either to consume or carry away with them, had wantonly shot down, to starve out the people and prevent them from making their crops. The stench in some places was unbearable; every few hundred yards we had to hold our noses or stop them with the cologne Mrs. Elzey had given us, and it proved a great* [benefit]*. The dwellings that were standing all showed signs of pillage, and on every plantation we saw the charred remains of the ginhouse and packing screw* [where cotton was prepared for market]*, while here and there lone chimney stacks, 'Sherman's sentinels,' told of homes laid in ashes. The infamous wretches!"*

—Eliza Andrews, a wealthy 24-year-old Georgian
traveling in the wake of Sherman's March

from Primary Sources Teaching Kit: *Civil War by Karen Baicker* (Scholastic, 2003)

HOSPITALS AND THE WOUNDED: CLARA BARTON
1864

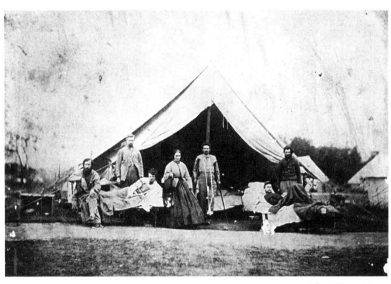

Atlanta History Center

"I saw crowded into one old sunken hotel, lying helpless upon its bare, wet, bloody floors, five hundred fainting men hold[ing] up their cold, bloodless, dingy hands as I passed, and beg[ging] me in Heaven's name for a cracker to keep them from starving (and I had none); or to give them a cup that they might have something to drink water from, if they could get it (and I had no cup and could get none); till I saw two hundred six-mule army wagons in a line, ranged down the street to headquarters, and reaching so far out on the Wilderness road that I never found the end of it; every wagon crowded with wounded men, stopped, standing in the rain and mud, wrenching back and forth by the restless, hungry animals all night from four o'clock in the afternoon till eight next morning and how much longer I know not. The dark spot in the mud under many a wagon, told only too plainly where some poor fellow's life had dripped out in those dreadful hours. . . .

Barton rushed to Washington to get the help from Sen. Henry Wilson, the chairman of a powerful Senate committee. Wilson, in turn, went to the War Department to get some action. Instead, officials there hemmed and hawed and said Wilson's information must be incorrect.

. . . Mr. Wilson assured them that the officers [at Fredericksburg] were not to be relied upon. . . . Still the Department doubted. It was then that he proved that my confidence in his firmness was not misplaced, as, facing his doubters he replies: "One of two things will have to be done—either you will send someone tonight with the power to investigate and correct the abuses of our wounded men at Fredericksburg, or the Senate will send someone tomorrow."

This threat recalled their scattered senses. . . .

. . . At two o'clock in the morning the Quartermaster-General and staff [headed off to Fredericksburg]. At noon the wounded men were fed from the food of the city and the houses were opened to the 'dirty, lousy soldiers' of the Union Army. . . .

Both railroad and canal were opened. In three days I returned with carloads of supplies.

from Primary Sources Teaching Kit: *Civil War by Karen Baicker (Scholastic, 2003)*

Bibliography of Professional Materials

Alvermann, D. E., & Phelps, S. E. (1998). *Content-area reading and literacy: Succeeding in today's diverse classrooms* (2nd ed.). Boston: Allyn and Bacon.

Beck, I. L., & McKeown, M. (2006). *Improving comprehension with questioning the author.* New York: Scholastic.

Dowhower, S. L. (1999). Supporting a strategic stance in the classroom: A comprehension framework for helping teachers help students to be strategic. *The Reading Teacher, 52*(7), 672–688.

Duke, N. K., & Pearson, P. D. (2002). Effective practices for developing reading comprehension. In A. E. Farstrup & S. J. Samuels (Eds.), *What research has to say about reading instruction* (3rd ed.). Newark, DE: International Reading Association.

Garner, R. (1992). Metacognition and self-monitoring strategies. In S. J. Samuels & A. E. Farstrup (Eds.), *What research has to say about reading instruction* (2nd ed.). Newark, DE: International Reading Association.

Gillet, J. W., & Temple, C. (2000). *Understanding reading problems: Assessment and instruction* (2nd ed.). New York: Longman.

Guthrie, J. T. (2004). Teaching for literacy engagement. *Journal of Literacy Research, 36*(1), 1–30.

Guthrie, J. T. & Wigfield, A. (2000). Engagement and motivation in reading. In *Handbook of reading research* (Vol. III). M. L. Kamil, P. B. Mosenthal, P. D. Pearson, & R. Barr (Eds.), Mahwah, NJ: Lawrence Erlbaum Associates.

Harvey, S. (1998). *Nonfiction matters: Reading, writing, and research in grades 3–8.* Portland, ME: Stenhouse.

Harvey, S., & Goudvis, A. (2000). *Strategies that work: Teaching comprehension to enhance understanding.* Portland, ME: Stenhouse.

Keene, E. O., & Zimmermann, S. (1997). *Mosaic of thought.* Portsmouth, NH: Heinemann.

Loewen, J. W. (1995). *Lies my teacher told me: Everything your American history textbook got wrong.* New York: The New Press.

Marzano, R. J. (2004). *Building background knowledge for academic achievement: Research on what works in schools.* Alexandria, VA: Association for Supervision and Curriculum Development.

Pearson, P. D. (2001). Life in the radical middle: A personal apology for a balanced view of reading. In R. F. Flippo (Ed.), *Reading researchers in search of common ground.* Newark, DE: International Reading Association.

Pearson, P. D., Roehler, L. R., Dole, J. A., & Duffy, G. G. (1992). Developing expertise in reading comprehension. In S. J. Samuels & A. E. Farstrup (Eds.), *What research has to say about reading instruction.* (2nd ed.). Newark, DE: International Reading Association.

Readence, J. E., Moore, D. W., & Rickelman, R. J. (2000). *Prereading activities for content-area reading and learning* (3rd ed.). Newark, DE: International Reading Association.

Robb, L. (2002). Multiple texts: Multiple opportunities for teaching and learning. *Voices from the middle, 9*(4), 28–32.

Robb, L. (2003). *Teaching reading in social studies, science, and math: Practical ways to weave comprehension strategies into your content-area teaching.* New York: Scholastic.

Robb, L. (2006). *Teaching reading: A complete resource for grades 4 and up.* New York: Scholastic.

Tierney, R. J., & Readence, J. E. (2000). *Reading strategies and practices: A compendium.* Boston: Allyn and Bacon.

Tomlinson, C. A. (1995). *How to differentiate instruction in mixed-ability classrooms.* New York: Basic Books.

Tomlinson, C. A. (1999). *The differentiated classroom: Responding to the needs of all learners.* Alexandria, VA: Association for Supervision and Curriculum Development.

Vacca, R. T., & Vacca, J. A. (2000). *Content-area reading: Literacy and learning across the curriculum* (6th ed.). New York: Longman.

Van Hoose, J. & Strahan, D. (1988). *Promoting harmony: Young adolescent development and school practices.* Columbus, OH: National Middle School Association.

Vaughn, J. L., & Estes, T. H. (1986). *Reading and reasoning beyond the primary grades.* Boston: Allyn and Bacon.

Wilhelm, J. D. (2002). *Action strategies for deepening comprehension.* New York: Scholastic.

Zarnowski, M. (2006). *Making sense of history: Using high-quality literature and hands-on experiences to build content knowledge.* New York: Scholastic.